BUSINESS AHA! TIPS

ON

SUCCESSFUL FUNDRAISING

BUSINESS AHA! TIPS

ON

SUCCESSFUL FUNDRAISING

Howard L. Smith

CC!
PRESS
BOISE STATE
UNIVERSITY

PUBLISHED BY CCI PRESS
of Boise State University

Managing editor: Stephanie Chism
Production Manager: Joanna Lui
Cover design by Paul Carew of Carew Co.

ISBN-13 978-0-9855305-6-3
BAT Series: Book 3

CCI Press - http://cobe.boisestate.edu/cci/cci-press/
BAT Series - http://cobe.boisestate.edu/cci/cci-press/bat-series/

Dedications

To all those generous people who care enough to give, so that others may benefit.

Acknowledgements

I would like to thank many dedicated colleagues in advancement I have worked with over the years; especially Rika Clement and Cheryl Larabee. You made all the difference in the world.

CONTENTS

Foreword

Leadership is becoming more demanding and complex, so constant learning is an important part of any leader's routine. At Packaging Corporation of America we are dedicated to continuous improvement, and we know that embracing creativity and innovation can help us improve performance. That's why Boise Inc., a Packaging Corporation of America company, is proud to build a partnership with the Centre for Creativity and Innovation, which is part of Boise State University's College of Business and Economics.

The Centre offers organizations the chance to generate insight and "aha" moments in many different ways. One of the most recent, and one that we at Boise Inc. are especially excited about, is the upcoming publications from the Centre's new CCI Press. These publications will help leaders gain insights efficiently and in ways that are immediately applicable, which are important attributes in our fast-paced world.

Boise Inc. is pleased to support the CCI Press's offering, the Business Aha! Tips series. This book offers insight and knowledge in an easy to read, easy to apply format.

I hope you take the ideas you learn from these books and use them to help your organization become a highly performing, highly creative one.

Virginia Aulin
Vice President, Human Resources
Communications and Corporate Affairs
Packaging Corporation of America

INTRODUCTION

On Bats

The logo of the *Business Aha! Tips* (BAT) books is a bat. The notion of a bat works for several reasons.

1. **Bats have good hearing.** Bats don't depend just on seeing, but also on their hearing systems. They emit ultrasonic sounds that produce echoes. When they compare the sounds they emit to the returning echoes, bats create detailed images of any prey, even in complete darkness. In business, managers must sound out strategies to analyze what may or may not work. They also must actively listen to customers, employees, and other stakeholders to make those practices work.

2. **Bats are fast.** They hunt insects by chasing them down while flying. In business, it is also important to move quickly to hit target markets.

3. **Bats are symbolic.** The Chinese link the bat with happiness and longevity, and these are good

characteristics to have in business as well. Bats are also associated with villains like Dracula and heroes like Batman. Managers, like bats, may be villains one day and heroes the next.

4. **Bats are adaptable.** Over fifty-two million years ago, bats such as the Onychonycteris had claws on all five fingers. Now bats have claws on only two fingers of each hand. Companies likewise need to evolve to adapt to new political, economic, market, and social conditions.

5. **Bats are active.** The bat logo, used throughout the book, designates places that ask you to act and apply the information you've just read.

6. **Bats look cool.** Enough said.

1

Setting the Stage

How is charitable fundraising going for your organization? This question is extremely relevant given the changing landscape of the economy. Unfortunately, many executives, staff members and trustees would be hard pressed to give an accurate answer because they are caught up in the frenzy of daily operations and intricate strategic planning. Others might reply that they have better things to do than go hustle donors for some spare change. A goodly number may claim that they have limited staff to rely on for support.

The world's economic crisis has brought devastating changes to philanthropy.[1] As a result, many nonprofit and non-governmental organizations struggle to attract essential resources; donations continue to be elusive; budgets are slashed deeply; and, meritorious goals go un-achieved or under-achieved due to insufficient financial support.[2] Cutting budgets is only a short-run answer. Eventually organizations relying on philanthropy must devise new diverse revenue streams or they perish. *This book is designed to prevent a death sentence from happening to your organization.*

An Ambitious Purpose

Successful Fundraising Aha! Tips captures the fine points and delicate nuances that make a significant difference in how effectively executives fulfill their advancement role. This book answers very basic, but essential, questions such as:

- How can executives become fruitful ambassadors for their organizations?
- What do they need to do to have a better chance of landing large donations and gifts?
- What ingenious strategies and tactics can they employ to raise large sums of money?
- What insightful suggestions are especially valuable when working with people of wealth?
- What does it take to raise millions of dollars?

As these questions suggest, this book was created to help executives and trustees make an order of magnitude difference in their fundraising efforts.

The imperative to think with great ingenuity that results in "Aha moments" is a consistent theme integral for addressing these issues above. Make no mistake about it, the fundamental operating assumptions underlying nonprofit programs and organizations have been irrevocably altered. Waiting around for the good old status quo to return is wishful thinking at best. The very fabric of philanthropy has been ripped asunder; now is the time to move rapidly forward while embracing imaginative approaches for acquiring essential resources. Compelling mission-critical changes in attitude, philosophy and behavior are needed from executives. Those who tarry in ramping up their inventiveness quotient will likely be passed by—or passed out of existence.

This book builds upon the work of Nancy K. Napier's *Insight: Encouraging Aha! Moments for Organizational Success* (Santa Barbara, California: Praeger, 2010) and a companion text by Gundars Kaupins and Nancy K. Napier, *Business Aha! Tips* (Boise, Idaho: CCI Press, 2012) developed at the Centre for Creativity and Innovation at Boise State University. As these background books imply, effective problem solving is highly dependent on formulating insights with ingenuity and imagination not only in defining problems but especially in developing and implementing unique solutions. *Successful Fundraising Aha! Tips* argues that a refreshing mindset is a prerequisite for today's fundraising environment. It is time to completely rethink the strategies and tactics typically employed in philanthropy.

A Winning Combination

Every executive has chores, assignments, expectations and duties that they do not like to complete yet are an essential part of doing business. High achievers tend to dwell more on huge results rather than minutiae associated with mundane tasks. These top performers simply live for big paybacks as well as the intrinsic satisfaction and extrinsic rewards they reap from landing noteworthy donations and gifts. They take great pride in encouraging targeted donors to find deeply meaningful connections with their organization or program. The objective is to ensure that donors want to be, demand to be, part of a collaborative effort to build something impressive, an initiative that is truly distinctive, and thus compels prospective donors to bring essential resources to the table.

Aha! Tip: High achievers tolerate the bulk of mundane tasks so that they can move on to the 20% of their effort that delivers 80% of final impressive results…such as fundraising.

Not surprisingly high performing executives tend to rely on well-designed strategies, structures and processes to get the humdrum tasks out of the way as quickly as possible. As Figure 1-1 indicates, in fundraising these basics generally include: prior preparation and planning as a prelude to prospect and donor interactions; setting the stage for successful engagement; maintaining a positive image; carefully orchestrating initial contacts; and, conducting business with the highest levels of courtesy, integrity and enthusiasm. These basics usually must be addressed *first* before focusing on ingenious strategies to cultivate lead prospects.

With game-plan basics covered, it is then a matter of ratcheting-up another level by addressing the following initiatives: building enduring relationships; imaginative thinking; capturing the attention of wealthy people; and, innovating beyond best practices to strategize for the new normal. These four initiatives spell the startling difference between true winners and also-rans. *Successful Fundraising Aha! Tips* drills down into these strategies to understand what it takes for executives to think and act differently in tough philanthropic environments. The fundamental idea is to approach fund raising in more imaginative and electrifying ways that excite donors.

Some Cautionary Caveats

Every effort has been made in the following pages to emphasize rigorously informative, energetically vibrant, and highly applicable examples both within *and outside* of the field of philanthropy. In fact, examples drawn from beyond fundraising are essential to thinking more ingeniously. These illustrations may appear to be amusing and somewhat humorous but they are not included solely for entertainment value. Each scenario conveys a very serious lesson.

Figure 1-1

Ingredients for Successful Fund and Friend Raising

Foundation Basics

- Prior preparation and planning as a prelude to prospect and donor interactions

- Setting the stage for successful engagement

- Maintaining a positive image

- Carefully orchestrating initial contacts

- Conducting business with the highest levels of courtesy, integrity, and enthusiasm

A Winning Combination for Successful Fund and Friend Raising

High-Performance Initiatives

- Building enduring relationships
- Imaginative thinking
- Capturing the attention of wealthy people
- Strategizing for our new normal

Read, reflect and chew on the ideas and concepts presented throughout this book. In the end there is no question that a revolution is needed in how executives think about friend and fund raising. This little guide should stimulate your creative juices and thus lead to successes that are wholly unanticipated, but justifiably deserved.

KEY AHA! POINTS

- Executives have an important and growing responsibility to lead fundraising efforts.
- The national and global economic recessions have adversely affected fundraising. More than ever donations are needed for capital projects and program development.
- Given the tough fundraising environment, efforts by executives and their organizations to increase donations will increasingly require imaginative thinking.
- A basic foundation of fundraising fundamental requires:
  o Prior planning to define goals and strategies
  o Setting the stage for success
  o Maintaining a positive image
  o Orchestrating initial contacts
  o Conducting business with integrity
- High fundraising performance requires a solid foundation of basics coupled with:
  o Building enduring relationships
  o Imaginative thinking
  o Capturing the attention of wealthy people
  o Strategizing for the new normal

Success Through Ingenuity

Nonprofit organizations face the hard fact that their fiscal needs are exceeding charitable donations even though giving has increased in the past three years.[3] Many have suffered dramatic decreases; plenty have winked out of existence.[4] Given these tumultuous times it is understandable that executives may be pessimistic about relying on fundraising to meet critical needs. Negativity can bubble to the surface in daily conversations:

- Without a doubt fundraising is in for more tough-sledding.
- We keep waiting for the economy to turn around but it just doesn't seem to gather strength.
- Too many hands are reaching for too few dollars; the pie shrank.
- We've tightened our belt and cut to the bone; there's no telling how we will meet the next round of budget cuts.
- It's a lost cause unless something miraculous happens.

Exactly when has it *never* been tough going in raising donations? With a few exceptions, even in the most robust economies the number of needy organizations generally exceeds available funds. There always seems to be competition to raise resource support.

Executives should seriously consider what message they send to trustees/board members and colleagues alike when they echo pundits of doom-and-gloom. The exact opposite can be persuasively argued. Now *is* a great time to be pursuing philanthropy, but not if executives think in the same old traditional ways about the economic environment and prospects for philanthropic giving.[5]

Aha! Tip:
Rethinking Opportunities for Philanthropy

- Today is a fantastic time to be an ambassador for any organization or program with a worthwhile cause.
- No context is too tough to gain support if imagination, cleverness, creativity, inventiveness and innovation are exercised.
- It is essential to remain open to unique, more innovative and clever fund raising strategies that can spell victory for your cause.

Let's walk through an interesting little vignette from outside philanthropy to begin stretching your thinking. On the surface this captivating story is pleasant enough. However, when all is said and done, the tale speaks volumes about creative thought processes—patterns of innovative thinking that are indispensable to "Aha moments" and to garnering support for worthwhile endeavors. Join me for a little stroll before starting a new day of work.

The "Aha" Parable of the Fox

Dawn's first meager light is merely an arcane theory as I leave my office bound for a daily saunter on our town's paved greenbelt path. These daybreak promenades offer a rich moment of calm before all hell breaks loose. Most folks have their morning rituals—newspapers, lattes, yoga, romance, whatever—and for me a brisk half-hour walk is a perfect way to start the day. I simply adore richly sensual scents lingering along our town's pastoral river mixed with a palpable chill that heralds an inevitable shift between seasons. Delicious quiet smothers well-trodden paths lining this blissful watercourse. It's almost quiet enough to think really BIG thoughts for the day.

Which way to go this morning? I could continue straight on the asphalt path to enjoy a half-mile swath of cottonwoods and willows, or I can turn left and spring over this bucolic river on a sharply arched concrete bridge. Magic waits on the other side of the bridge in the form of towering sequoia trees spread like stars on a velvet green canvas of grass. These sequoias may still be around another 1,500 years from now given their location by this river's cooling breath and abundant moisture.

Swinging to the left I begin rising on the bridge's arc. One-hundred feet or so and I'll be on the other side. Spread along round-river-rock infested sandbars bracketing this river swarms of Canada geese and mallards rise for a dawn chorus. Their quacking, honking, yapping ruckus fills the night as it bleeds toward sunrise. It's enough to make me chuckle. They can't seem to keep it down. First one set of Canada geese chases off some interloper who inadvertently stepped into their perceived territory on the north bank. The intruder takes flight to the other side. Then, four mallards initiate a peck-fest on the south, pitch-black riverbank swapping more than a few disagreeable quacks. A few luminescent feathers are left floating in the air, gradually going to ground as everyone rearranges themselves in neutral zones.

Eight paces up the bridge, roughly a quarter of the way across, I gain enough elevation to see to the other side as well as a totally unanticipated surprise coming toward me. A buff fluffy red fox is headed in my direction. This is a vibrantly healthy metro fox; one that is nearly three-feet long appears to weigh some 20 pounds and whose monstrous tail plume is at least two-feet long. Its brilliant coat literally shimmers.

We both grind to a screeching halt.

I stare at the fox and it stares right back at me. Conclusion: neither of us is going to tuck tail and run the other way.

I wait perhaps 30 seconds and the fox stands its ground not budging an inch, but also not making any aggressive moves.

At the end of those 30 seconds the fox turns it head to see behind it. Like me, it has progressed roughly 25% of the way across the bridge. The last thing it wants is to be pinned in by someone coming behind it. The river is a good 30 feet below…too far for either of us to bail out.

No one is coming.

I glance behind to see if anyone is coming that way.

Nothing.

We return to our stalemate.

I decide to make the next move.

I flatten against the bridge's steel railing as unobtrusive as I can make myself and look over to the fox while softly saying, "Go ahead, I'm not going to do anything stupid."

The fox looks behind itself once, twice, three times and then decides it will trust my intentions.

Come on," I almost whisper

Slowly, but purposefully without changing stride, the fox trots my way. It keeps its head pointed straightforward and jogs gradually past my flattened body at a semi-sauntering pace. As it reaches me it continues looking straight-ahead and then quickly shifts it eyes in my direction to steal a glance without altering its pace.

A couple of seconds later it is off the bridge and pauses to look back at me. I simply nod and it continues about its business. I'm free to pass over the bridge and to luxuriate through sequoia-land on the other side.

A chance encounter with a red fox lights my soul on fire. The remainder of the day I float along buoyed by this spiritual connection.

Aha Lessons about Friend and Fund Raising

Some will conclude that I am making too much of the fox encounter; that it was not some pinnacle kumbaya-moment where human and fellow mammal plumbed the philosophical depths of life or the cosmos. Sorry...I tend to read a lot into a special exchange like this. Granted the fox and I didn't carry on a lengthy discourse; but, two beings did clearly communicate with each other.

Others may ask, "What in the world does all of this have to do with successful fundraising?" From my way of thinking, there are five key lessons that can be derived from this short scenario.

Aha Tip:
Five Key Lessons from the Parable of the Fox
1. Imagination Creates Positive Outcomes
2. Correctly Read Intentions
3. Build Trust
4. Reap Unanticipated Returns
5. Touch another Being

Each of these lessons is unabashedly germane to attaining victory when it comes to fundraising.

Imagination Creates Positive Outcomes

I think it is fair to say that the majority of people hearing about my confrontation with the red fox would have reacted quite differently. A typically human reaction when encountering any opposing mammal with a sharp set of teeth is to either back off or, more likely, try to scare the fox away. In fact this is precisely what wildlife experts counsel for altercations with North America's most prevalent life-threatening carnivores and omnivores like black bears and mountain lions.[4] Look big. Act tough. Talk trash. Defend yourself if necessary. Just don't try this with grizzly bears.

The fox could easily have been chased off, but what would I have gained by doing that? Continued on my way with a macho swagger about how I taught it a lesson? That sort of false bravado is too prevalent in the workplace.

By doing the exact opposite of what most people would do—the so-called "typical" reaction—conditions were nurtured for a very magical moment. I was willing to be the submissive bridge buddy and to let the fox determine what was going to happen next. It obviously had a big agenda on the other side of the bridge. Perhaps kits were waiting unprotected. Maybe the fox had a clandestine rendezvous pre-arranged. It's possible that the fox was avoiding a predator. Likely the fox knew about some food source that might be available at this time of early morning. Whatever the causal variable or factors; that fox wanted to get to the other side of the bridge and I was in its way.

By not panicking and thinking quickly about the options available to me, I thoroughly enjoyed a little dance that most people never have the chance to consider. A modest amount of ingenious thinking—an "Aha moment"—

created a very positive outcome. And, it is precisely inventiveness of this sort that is so vitally needed in fundraising.

Please remember that if you are not experienced in responding to wildlife the best option is usually to back away and leave any animal alone for your safety, the safety of those with you and protection of the wild animal.

Correctly Read Intentions

Much of my decision rested on reading the situation correctly. If the fox was standing its ground with bared white fangs, drooling foamy saliva and a guttural snarling growl, it would have been easy to know what to do next. But, the fox wasn't exhibiting any alarming signs. The fox showed not a smidgen of aggression. On-the-other-hand, it also did not display submissive behavior. There were no flattened ears, drooping head, tail tucked between its legs while covering/protecting its rear-end, or crouching posture. The fox stood there without intimidation, without aggression and with a hint of a question on its mind.

I do not have a tremendous amount of experience in reading foxes' facial expressions or body posture. Perhaps I have only seen a good two-dozen-plus foxes in my life. But, I do have inordinately vast experience in trying to read the facial expressions and body posture from thousands of encounters with two-legged mammals. And what that historical data bank told me was to trust this being…even if it was a wily old fox.

I correctly read the fox's intentions. Now I could have been wrong and gotten bitten. That's happened to me plenty of times with two-legged mammals of the human kind. Nonetheless from all of these thousands of experiences I have tried to learn about reading the fine nuances of mammalian postures, facial expressions, and body images. It seems to me that this challenge is exactly what separates successful executive fund raisers from the run-of-the-mill. Those executives who get it right are more likely to also bring in more than their fair share of the resources.

Build Trust

Most people, most donors, will reserve their trust until after they have gotten to know someone. Few will give you the benefit of the doubt by beginning with a trusting relationship. They may not show their skepticism, but they are not going to let on that they have great suspicion about your intentions. Trust is generally acquired the hard way. You have to earn it, and justifiably so.

Brother/sister fox and I faced a dilemma. Neither of us was going to get to where we wanted to go unless we trusted the other to not do something stupid. Undoubtedly this was a metro fox with many experiences from intentionally engaging a wide spectrum of humans. It probably had an impressive history of encounters that helped it take a reading on the large two-legged standing 50 feet away. Moreover, from this experiential base, the fox was able to read my posture, facial expression and body image (i.e., willingness to flatten against the bridge railing). Everything about me spoke loudly of predictability: "He's not showing any signs of aggression."

By remaining in place I let the fox have the opportunity to test the waters. Perhaps it thought that it might close the distance between us by half to see what my reaction would be. Undoubtedly it set a bail-out point where a change in posture would result in retreat. Whatever its thought processes, the fox became predisposed to trusting me. Everything about me read: "trust this guy not to do something stupid." If the fox was wrong; it could run away with or without biting me first. More likely trust was buoyed by prior experience with humans that informed the fox that it was quick and agile enough to escape.

In many respects this dance about trust is exactly what executives do when they build relationships with prospects and donors. One false move and the relationship is retarded. As foxes know, trust is never given; it is earned.

Reap Unanticipated Returns

When I ran into the red fox on the bridge I wasn't exactly thinking about the possibility that I would suddenly intersect any sort of wildlife. Admittedly I have seen more than my share of feral animals during these early morning forays: mink, beaver, bald eagles, otters, herons, elk, and students stumbling back to dorms after what appeared to have been wild nights. I had no pre-planned motive for intercepting any fauna. I was simply taking a walk. As a result I wasn't expecting *anything* when I ran into the fox.

Reactions to the red fox incident came quite naturally because I did not have any particular ulterior motive in mind. I innocently did what I thought was the correct thing to do at such a moment. I can honestly say that I expected absolutely nothing in return for flattening against the bridge railing like Garfield-on-glass. Perhaps that is why I reaped unanticipated returns from the fox's passing.

Interestingly, this innocent motive—focusing only on an express concrete action—that produced an unanticipated reward is frequently observed in fundraising. I am continually amazed at the unexpected niceties donors and prospects shower on organizations when executives cultivate them with the uppermost honesty and transparency. Sometimes the return is larger than the express cultivation goal.

In retrospective the red fox did not have to hesitate once it reached the other side of the bridge; *but, it did*. It could have just kept on rocking and rolling toward whatever destination that it had in mind; but, the fox did not. It took the time, however slight, to communicate in its fashion with a fellow being. I find that remarkable. A red fox had more manners and consideration than we often find among our own species. Conceivably I'm too much of a romantic and have anthropomorphized too much. Reach your own conclusion; for me the fox wanted to communicate something positive about the event.

The take-away for me from this encounter is reinforcement of always approaching prospects and donors with the most honorable, sincere and transparent intentions. Take the high road and you may be surprised at the unanticipated returns you reap.

Touch another Being

I learned another lesson from meeting the red fox. That critter provided more interaction with me than most people whom I normally pass on the bridge. The fox repeatedly acknowledged my presence through eye contact. Most folks pass by without as much as an upward glance or head-nod, much less a pleasant word or "grunt."

Isn't that a wonderful realization to take away from this early dawn encounter? Two sentient beings could have passed like ships in the night. Instead they communicated loudly and clearly even though they don't speak the same language. How powerful is that?

This opportunity to metaphorically touch others in positive ways during cultivation and solicitation processes is easily overlooked as a richly rewarding aspect of fundraising. Such closeness and deep sharing may happen only occasionally. Executives have a chance to get to a higher level in their personal interactions which is a phenomenally attractive aspect of fundraising. What's more, like my bumping into the red fox, it isn't even necessary to say one word. Perhaps it is the gesture of standing up when meeting someone for the first time, opening a door, or sending a thank you note. Remember the reward you might receive for small, but highly significant, actions that tell others that their humanness is important to you.

Roadmap to Results

Few other professions may offer as many opportunities to help other people while at the same time enriching one's personal and professional lives as the fundraising profession. Nonetheless, rewards do not suddenly materialize without an added measure of effort and ingenious experimentation.

Successful Fundraising Aha! Tips argues for a fresh perspective. Executives should realize that the science of fundraising may tend to overwhelm the importance of good old-fashioned one-on-one relationship building. Paradoxically, I have witnessed first-hand about how colleagues can get so caught up in "doing things according to the book" and "following best practices" that they seemingly forget about their mission in the first place, which is increasing funds raised and expanding the base of friends who might bring resources and influence to bear on behalf of a program or organization.

It is appropriate to remember the red fox. Think differently in how you approach donors and prospects and you too may experience outcomes that you never dreamed possible.

KEY AHA! POINTS

- Executives can choose to give up in the face of a difficult philanthropy environment or they can rethink the manner in which they go about fundraising.

- The gist of deep knowledge about effectively working with donors suggests 5 important Aha lessons that were exemplified by "The Parable of the Fox":
  - o Imagination creates positive outcome
  - o Correctly read donor intention.
  - o Build trust with donor.
  - o Reap unanticipated returns through deeper relationships with donor.
  - o Touch another being and cement a meaningful relationship.

- Unbridled patterns of innovative thinking are indispensable to garnering support for worthwhile endeavors.

A Winning Game Plan

How do a few executives consistently achieve stellar results? Close examination of high performers inevitably demonstrates that they are very efficient in following a winning game plan which has been progressively honed over the years.[6] They religiously adhere to a plan by strictly implementing basic fundamentals in a crisp and concise fashion. They know exactly what must be done every day no matter what the costs. Moreover, they accept the reality that they too must slog through all of the daily minutiae while at the same time minimizing the extent to which such detail derails their laser-sharp focus.

High performers diligently take care of the 80% of those tasks, responsibilities and activities, *the basis for a winning game plan*, that only produce 20% of their results. *And*, they manage them as expeditiously as possible. That doesn't mean they like to do these (often) mind-numbing assignments. They simply recognize that it is easier to not overly grouse about these expectations, but to wrap them up so that they can move on to more promising time investments. In many cases they have learned experientially that if you take short-cuts you probably have to pay a higher price in the end by repeating or re-doing some of the tasks. It is all a matter of balance.

> **Aha! Tip:** Try to short-cut the day-to-day responsibilities and it will eventually catch up with you.

Architecture of a Winning Plan

Successful fundraisers generally follow a predictable, basic model that predisposes them for high performance. As shown in Figure 3-1, they: undertake sufficient preparation and planning; set the stage; maintain a positive image; carefully orchestrate initial contacts; and, conduct business with the highest levels of courtesy, integrity and enthusiasm. These five elements capture the majority of a high performing executive's game plan. Many executives add a few bells and whistles that are unique to them or that reflect their particular style and philosophy. However, it is important to recognize that by finely executing the preceding elements, most executives can raise their game to a substantially higher level. Let's briefly walk through each of these basic points.

Undertaking Sufficient Preparation and Planning

The science portion of fundraising tends to congregate on the front end—efforts are made to identify promising qualified prospects for a campaign or cultivation initiative. Bless those staff members who are skilled in rummaging through electronic databases and public documents.

Figure 3-1

Five Steps toward a Winning Game Plan

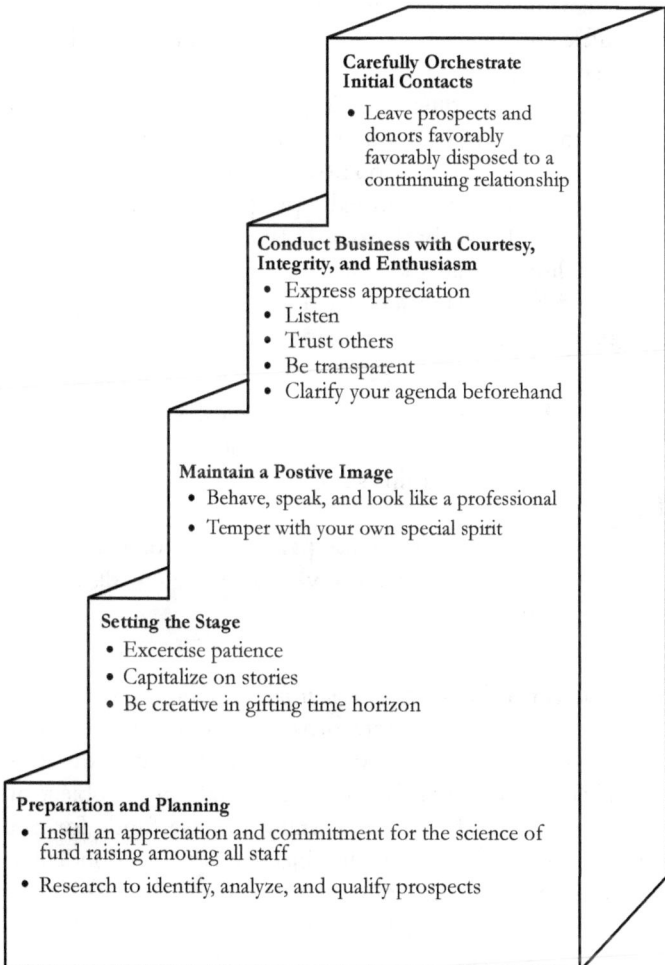

Carefully Orchestrate Initial Contacts

- Leave prospects and donors favorably favorably disposed to a contininuing relationship

Conduct Business with Courtesy, Integrity, and Enthusiasm

- Express appreciation
- Listen
- Trust others
- Be transparent
- Clarify your agenda beforehand

Maintain a Postive Image

- Behave, speak, and look like a professional
- Temper with your own special spirit

Setting the Stage

- Excercise patience
- Capitalize on stories
- Be creative in gifting time horizon

Preparation and Planning

- Instill an appreciation and commitment for the science of fund raising amoung all staff
- Research to identify, analyze, and qualify prospects

Highly driven prospect research staff inevitably spy minute, but important leads in newspapers, magazines, web searches, and similar sources. Research staff members who are particularly gifted have a penchant for ferreting out sleepers. These are the prospects who possess enormous potential to give (and who may even have generously contributed to various causes in a low key way) but who have remained out of the limelight.

Sufficient preparation and planning begins with this coveted background research. Executives need to acquire as solid an understanding of each prospect as possible. When identifying, qualifying and making first contact with any major donor, my goal is to know as much as possible about that person's life from all perspectives and on all dimensions. These background data enable me to better frame a life portrait or a profile of what a person values most and how likely they will resonate with my program's initiative or organization's mission.

Aha! Tip: First, frame a logical story of how a person has achieved success in life and how that life connects in some vigorous way with your organization.

Second, sleuth for parallel links or convenient intersections that serve as engaging discussion points.

A person's life story is essential to understand because our goal is to help educate prospects (and donors) about how their life is synonymous with that of our organization/program. Unfortunately the primary object of our desire is *not* about our yearning to raise funds for our particular cause. The ultimate objective is to build indelible relationships between our entity and a vast cadre of supporters. Is there any better path to achieve this intimacy than clearly demonstrating that the life a donor has been living and what she/he is living for is for all intents and purposes exactly (or in close approximation to) what an organization is all about?

Setting the Stage

Once all of the background work is complete, essential analysis has identified promising prospects, and we have garnered a wide array of intelligence about their personal capacities, proclivities and preferences, it is time to set the stage for cultivation. This is akin to the same fine-tuning that happens before embarking on any family holiday vacation. By prior preparation and planning we know when, where, and how we will travel. It is then a matter of adding fine touches to ensure that our experience is distinctive. This may mean making dinner reservations at a swanky restaurant; arranging for a guided tour of an historic building or landmark attraction; bringing along jet skis to power around a lake; or, any of thousands of small initiatives that add up to make a trip unique and distinctive. Setting the stage is all about those details that predispose the cultivation of donors to success.

AHA! CASE INSIGHT

Our CEO called to let me know that I had an opportunity to make a short personal presentation to a wealthy couple. They were considering donating $1 million to our institution and a competitor across town...in short; they wanted to hear about two or three of possibilities before making a decision. We speculated that the competition planned on making a request for their pet program involving medical technology. I knew immediately which of our programs that I wanted to highlight, but I needed to discover more about the donors.

A staff member searched our database. In their late 70's, this couple had recently benefitted from the sale of their construction-related business. Now they needed a tax break, but they did not have a good idea about how they wanted to spend their money to derive this advantage. Most of the intelligence we were gathering suggested that these folks would not be excited about our competitor's core competence in healthcare technology even though their business increasingly relied on technological improvements to raise productivity. Word was coming in that they were especially supportive of traditional values.

Assembling all of this information, as well as insights I accumulated over the years about our competition, I began to set the stage. I knew that the competition was absolutely gaga about medical technology and consequently would not speak without a computer-aided presentation. The competition would think that they were wowing these donors with a sophisticated presentation; but I counted on the fact that the prospective donors would not necessarily agree. They would not perceive any special value in a glossy electronic presentation. I reasoned that the donors would be repulsed by our competitor's slick presentation skills. For my part I decided to eschew an electronic medium and further I decided to go completely without any handouts. My presentation would consist of talking face-to-face in plain terms.

Our big day arrived and I asked them to join me at the conference table. It was just me looking directly at them across the table. Over the next five minutes I went directly to the point. I told them about our program and how we had grown and in the process had received recognition as one of the top 15 programs in the world—I repeated "in the world." Then, with a smidgen of detail I told them about how $1 million would be used to take us to the top 5 programs in the world; we would be one of the pinnacle programs on this globe.

With each and every word I looked directly in their eyes and made certain to switch my gaze from one to the other. I did not want them thinking I was being aggressive by staring at them. My little soliloquy was over in a matter of moments; I answered a question and thanked them for giving me a chance to present to them.

Four days later I was informed that the donors decided to invest in my program…it was a humbling lesson in properly setting the stage for success. Technology is a huge advantage, but sometimes the stage is better set by attending to the predilections and preferences of donor prospects.

Although the precise strategies I utilize to set the stage are primarily contingent on the characteristics of each prospect or donor, three considerations continually surface as an essential foundation. They include patience, compelling stories, and prudent gifting time horizon.

Patience

One word captures the essence of setting the stage toward successful fundraising—patience. Successful fundraising is all about patience; patience in building relationships; patience in stewarding donors toward additional gifts; patience in waiting for the proper moment to make a solicitation; and, patience in going back to methodical cultivation strategies when a request aborts or ends on a polite pushback until a later date.

> **Aha! Tip:** Too many want to raise the quick buck and then move on to something greater waiting down the road. To them only one word is appropriate: patience.

Each and every donor is different. Their successful cultivation and solicitation requires a specially tailored approach that acknowledges their values (i.e., concept of the desirable), likes and dislikes, affinity toward an organization (particularly its mission and needs), fiscal abundance, giving options, life planning, family, and the whole host of personal traits and experiences that indicate when and to what extent they will be open to giving. For some donors it is appropriate to move quickly ahead, while for others an entire sequence of gifts must be planned for. They may start small with a preliminary gift to test how their resources will be used before building to larger and eventually legacy-level gifts. Others give one-time and that is it. Still others give and then fade away as their interests change over time—a reality that you cannot control much less manage in any operative sense of the word. They simply change due to unforeseen pressures. Through it all you must be patient.

Convincing Stories

Every executive should be highly versed in legendary tales and persuasive stories that help prospects and donors to visualize what an organization does best and what it is aspiring to accomplish over the long-run. I have discovered that such anecdotes personalize and nurture understanding of an organization's redeeming aspects. They assist in vividly conveying the challenges that an organization is struggling to overcome; hence the requisite need for resources to accomplish a task.

AHA! CASE INSIGHT

On a dark fall night I was enjoying a donor reception with about fifty dedicated souls. We were assembled under a large tent that was doing a passable job of keeping the cooling night breezes at bay. Admittedly, I was a bit too focused on noshing the delightful barbeque hors d'oeuvres while enjoying a delightful glass of wine. Folks were rotating from one little cell of four-to-five alumni to another sharing amusing stories about their time at the college I represented and laughing about some of the truly idiotic things they were bold enough to do at an earlier age. In all the vibes were extraordinarily mellow.

Then, I felt a tap on my shoulder. I stopped midway in a conversation and turned to greet a diminutive young lady who introduced herself as a recent graduate. She was positively brimming with enthusiasm; happy beyond all measure. She went on to relate a joyous story. She was born in Mexico and along with her five brothers immigrated to the United States and obtained citizenship. Despite her encouragement, she was the only sibling to earn a college degree while working almost full-time. She wanted to share with me that she had earlier in the year landed a fabulous public accounting job which she attributed to her education at our institution. As a single parent of two children she was adamant that they would also earn their higher education degrees.

How much better does it get? Here was a first generation college graduate who pulled herself up by her bootstraps. Not content to live off the system, she worked diligently to earn a good education and to secure a job. This was one graduate who would make certain that her children also graduated from college. Such a story speaks volumes to donors that may want to donate a scholarship to single parents. I used this illustration often in the subsequent years to help potential donors understand how important a donation can be in influencing not only one student, but successive generations of students.

Substitute the word "client" for the word "student" and it should be readily apparent how universally applicable this example is. The names and faces may change, but the substance of the idea does not—every entity can identify convincing stories that underscore how they have deeply touched a patient or client.

Creativity in Gifting Time Horizon

"If you don't fly first class, your children will," our extremely wealthy prospect observed as we walked side-by-side toward this posh resort's massive wooden doors leading to an absolute fairy-tale-land restaurant waiting inside.

Stop for a moment and think carefully about what this prospect had confided in me.

Essentially he was communicating that as far as he and his wife were concerned, they loved their children dearly and wanted to leave them legacy inheritances, BUT they also wanted to enjoy the largesse of an exceedingly successful career. Although I could not rule out a healthy donation in the short-run, all signs pointed to a better probability of capturing a substantial planned gift. The longer time horizon of planned gifts provide a mechanism for many donors to pursue short-run spending while protecting a corpus of funds that will support larger giving goals. My prospect did not have any trouble with waiting to gift my organization a large sum of his resources, why should I be disappointed in his time horizon?

Successful fund raising hinges on adapting ourselves to donors' time horizons. From my perspective, I rather have a gift in the short-run, but I will certainly be ecstatic if I only receive one for the long-run. To me it is intriguing to speculate about the benefit an organization will experience 5, 10 even 20 years down the road when a planned gift finally matures.

Aha! Tip: Longer-time-horizon-gifts function as a form of legacy that an executive can leave for an organization.

A fluctuating economy offers a perfect environment to think creatively about gift time horizons. In adverse economic times, prospects and donors are more comfortable with spreading their gifts over a longer timeframe. This leads me to envision stages or steps of giving that ultimately create the critical gift mass essential to achieving our fundamental goal. Consider the following illustration.

Assume that Program Q costs $150,000 in annual operating costs. A normal desire is to create an endowment that will perpetually cover this expense level. Further assume that the benefitting organization earns 5% on endowed accounts. Thus, it needs $3 million in endowed corpus to cover the annual operating expenses.

Three million dollars is a large sum of money to raise, especially in a tough economy. Rather than go after the entire sum, it may be more promising to cultivate a prospect over a creative time horizon. Step #1 is to cover the annual operation costs for a short period of three years. I may prefer that the prospect commits $3 million right then and there; but I am willing to delay a large request because the probabilities favor a rejection and my prospect will possibly walk away. A commitment of $150,000 for three years is certainly reason to celebrate because of the opportunity cost implications for budgeting. There is (annually) $150,000 that can be internally reallocated for other purposes. Plus, the prospect is predisposed to consider additional gifts in the future.

By the middle of year three in this scenario (i.e., two and one-half years after receiving the gift) it is time to discuss Step #2—repeating the initial gift, or establishing the endowment (or portion thereof). Note that the discussion is much easier because there is a history of giving, and it is most likely that in the worst case scenario the donor will re-up for another three year commitment. There are almost three years to excite my donor about Program Q, its staff and their inspiring programmatic results. In effect, I have established a predisposition for success. If the economy is still horrendous, or if the donor has had a financial set-back, then the option of renewing the three year $150,000 pledge may be the most favorable option. If the donor and/or economy have experienced good fiscal trends, then a request for establishing the $3 million endowment, *or a reasonable portion thereof* (e.g., $1 million, $1.5 million or $2 million), becomes the intended solicitation.

The next steps hinge completely on how the donor's financial situation matures. The important lesson is to be creative in thinking about time horizons. Use imagination when times are tough to secure short-run operating funding and to build long-run endowed funding.

Maintaining a Positive Image

Maintaining a positive image is especially critical to successful fund and friend raising. It is a 24 hour/7 days a week proposition to maintain a positive image. No fundraising effort can stand the setbacks that arise from inattention to how staff behave, speak and look in setting a professional image.

AHA! CASE INSIGHT

We were recruiting a new staff member. When my assistant scheduled me for a luncheon meeting the next day with the latest very marketable candidate, it seemed like I could go through the scenario in my sleep—get to know the individual over lunch, hear about the initial results after vetting with other staff during the morning interviews, and wait for the final tally by the end of the day. My colleagues were very good at informally coming to consensus before I was ever involved in the game. It was a very efficient process that in the final analysis had landed top talent.

That evening as I drove home from work I ran into a snarl of traffic that made my mood downright miserable. I was listening to National Public Radio about the high price of gas and world-wide economics that had driven it there. To make matters worse I was following a monstrous yellow Humvee with a license plate that read "HotStuf." This insensitive lout was precisely the reason for our problem in the first place. Driving this macho machine only made matters worse for all of us who couldn't afford such ostentatious conspicuous consumption. I fumed at this idiot, following behind him at 5 mph for several miles of interminable traffic jam. Certainly tomorrow had to be better.

Lunch went exactly as planned. This particular candidate was very savvy and displayed all of the right interactions during this informal meeting with six of my staff. However, the deeper we went into the interview, the more my credibility detector was riding on maximum because the performance was so well orchestrated. Something seemed amiss, but I just could not put my finger on it. Was it a lack of sincerity? Or, did I just feel like he was telling me what he wanted me to hear? My intuition told me to be careful, but I also had to admit that his performance was very smooth.

We gradually exited the restaurant as a group, and I went last as I sorted the papers from paying another recruiting bill. As I walked out the door I watched in semi-horror as a huge yellow Humvee sped around the parking lot and headed in the same direction as our office complex. I was dumbfounded, but clever enough to race to my car and begin a mad dash to see if I couldn't make it there before the Humvee did; assuming it was headed there.

In record time I made it to our office and captured a spot where I could look out a one-way window on our parking lot. Seconds later, in pulled a gi-normous yellow Humvee with license plate reading "HotStuf." Bingo.

Perhaps I should say "Blingo." Out of the vehicle jumped the candidate I had shared lunch with. What a difference 24 hours can make. He marched hurried to his next engagement, while I made a late appointment for that day with the person to whom he would report. This was going to be a very interesting recruiting debriefing.

Four hours later, I met with the soon-to-be supervisor.

"Hi, thanks for stopping by," I led off. "What is everyone saying about the candidate?" The potential supervisor spent 20 minutes extolling the virtues of our candidate: super experience; comes from a sales background; sounds very sincere about promoting our organization; huge professionally sophisticated appearance and demeanor; knows persons "X" and "Y" in our community who are people of great wealth; has a couple of other offers he is considering; and, was very impressed by you (i.e., me)." The last comment was obviously a throw-away.

"So, what do you think," I reply, "Do we hire him?"

This potential supervisor was only going to stick a big toe in the water. Something I had said; how I had said it; or, my posture, must have given me away." The potential supervisor decided to play it safe: "Well, first, what do you think of him?" Good question. So I answered it with another question. "Did you notice anything out-of-the ordinary with this candidate?"

The potential supervisor mulled it over for a few seconds and then stuck his entire foot in the water. "He seemed to be, how do we say, highly accessorized." "He had on a lot of ostentatious jewelry that made me wonder why he needed this job if he could afford such baubles."

I was extremely pleased to know I wasn't the only one who had noticed.

I then shared my little experience with the Humvee from the previous night and my little race back to our office. We agreed that "HotStuf" was absolutely the wrong message we wanted to send to our donors and prospects. Imagine how a conservative person of wealth would feel after watching our potential new staff member ride off in the sunset with a cloud of exhaust and slap in your face via the license plate.

Maintaining a positive image is especially critical to successful fund and friend raising. It is a 24 hour/7 days a week proposition to maintain a positive image. No fundraising effort can stand the setbacks that arise from inattention to how staff behave, speak and look in setting a professional image.

By the same token, I also question dressing too well or too stylishly. I always shoot for a professional image, but I never want to be seen or interpreted as competition for donors, prospects, or bosses. In the past I had one board member who was a real clothes aficionado. Whenever I met with him I purposefully tried to look inconspicuous. He did not want competition given his sartorial flair; and, there was no way that I could possibly afford the high thread count clothes from the finest New York, Paris and Rome haut couture purveyors hanging off his shoulders.

Be you, but be professional.

Conducting business with the highest levels of courtesy, integrity and enthusiasm

Our challenge is to conduct business with the utmost level of courtesy, integrity and enthusiasm. An inspiring goal is for executives to approach their responsibilities with a strong measure of elegance and grace in a world that had been dumbed-down as far as social interactions and philanthropic relationships are concerned. A solid base can be established from the following ideas. These suggestions cost little to implement, but provide a phenomenal return because they add a patina of distinctiveness to those who make the effort.

Express Appreciation

It is nearly impossible to overly express appreciation. In this entitlement-oriented world it is sadly more the exception than the rule that people have the courtesy to say, "thank you." Above all, make certain that the person(s) making a gift completely understands your gratitude. This is the rudimentary basis upon which lasting relationships are based.

> **Aha! Tip:** Follow the Rule of Two: make certain that appreciation is expressed both verbally and in writing. Redundancy ensures that at least one of these overtures will be heard and appreciated.

You would think that expressing appreciation is easy in a contemporary digital world. But, I believe that the matter is made more difficult by the endless onslaught of information that passes our tweets, posts, blogs, in-boxes, and other receptacles. We are inundated by overtures and as a result tend to quickly discard what may otherwise be important messages. Redundancy is an insurance policy to make certain that donors do not receive the wrong message, or any message for that matter.

Listen

Listening is perhaps the most essential skill any executive can cultivate whether as leader or fundraiser. The old adage goes that we should listen twice as much as we speak; that is why we have one tongue and two ears. For most people it takes a great effort to remain focused on listening rather than speaking. That may be the result of attempting to fill up silence with words—silence can be deafening when in the company of another. In other cases, excessive talking is primarily the result of ego gone awry.

Some people *do* know it all; at least they think so judging by their behavior. And, how boring can that become? Remember how people speak so enthusiastically about someone who is a good listener? That someone could be you.

Aha! Tip:

<u>Basic Ingredients to Becoming a Good Listener</u>

1. Keep in mind that listening to another person is equivalent to giving a gift. A receptive listener is a rare gem to discover.

2. Show respect by letting someone else talk first and then focus intently on what they have to say to you.

3. Look completely and continually into the other person's face in a polite and non-confrontation manner. They will welcome your gaze in return by sharing intimate details.

4. Concentrate on hearing what another person is telling you. It is one thing to listen and another to fully concentrate and process the other person's conversation.

5. Remember that it takes two people to carry on a conversation. Look for opportunities to interject your thoughts and to politely seek clarification when the discussion becomes confusing.

6. Engage the other person by guiding the discussion. Explain what perspective, insights or opinion you are interested in hearing and then let them speak without excessive interruption.

7. If you want to dominate a conversation then go talk to your dog or cat. They will listen for hours without interference.

Treat others as you wish to be treated

Every person, every family, has its stories of triumph and tragedy. Few of us are immune to the highs and lows of fortune. As we go about our jobs of raising friends and funds it is important to keep in mind that we all share in this thing we call life. I believe that it is appropriate to commit to leaving those that we touch better off for our passing through. Thus when it comes to someone who is in ill-health, who is hounded by a history of personal trial, or someone whose heart is broken for the loss of a loved one, it is appropriate that we treat them as we would wish to be treated. That is known as the "Golden Rule," and it is a lesson that we should remember daily as we serve as ambassadors for our profession and our organizations.

AHA! CASE INSIGHT

My client was in the midst of a forty-five minute monologue about his experience as a young man with my organization. At that far distant moment it had been a heady time for him as he freely experimented in life. His appetite for new experiences was large, prodigiously enormous, even if he was slight in stature. This was not the first time that he had shared these sentiments with me. And, he was obviously going to replay these scenarios one more time without even a thought as to whether he had told me about them in the past. That was fine by me; he deserved attention given his failing health.

Not too many days later I would be listening as another friend of our organization relived those days when he lost a multi-million dollar fortune. One moment he was retired for life and the next, after a call from his investment advisor, he was dead broke. The pain in his voice was palpable even though he recovered and grew a new fortune of such vastness that few of us could conceive of what it would be like to be so wealthy—a multi-millionaire by world standards. Yet, in those distant years, there was no love for a multi-millionaire who was down on his luck and soon to be on the streets.

Later that week I would sup with a most elegant and fabulously wealthy lady who lost her spouse to an insidious disease. She would always have the financial wherewithal to live a comfortable life, but her soul was morose without her husband. In many respects one could tell that she was just marking time until she would be with him. It was as if she was never truly there in person. Her body was present. She fixed her gaze on you as conversation flitted from one topic to another. But in reality she just was somewhere else with him.

Everyone has a story to tell and pain to endure…treat others with respect because someday it will be you sharing a sad story.

Be transparent

There is little that is more aggravating than knowing another person has a hidden agenda, and watching them think that they are pulling the wool over your eyes. In the final analysis there are no secrets in raising friends and funds. Truth will eventually surface. Consequently it makes good business sense to be transparent in all matters of prospect and donor relationships.

AHA! CASE INSIGHT

One year due to a spousal moment of miscommunication, we reserved a non-refundable two-night visit to one of the West's swankiest resorts in Jackson Hole. I had always been looking forward to staying at this lodge and now would finally be my chance. Unfortunately, my spouse's employer changed work schedules and she ended up working on the days in question. I had already sunk some three-thousand dollars into the little respite and my wife was tapped out of annual leave. But, I knew how that investment might offer a good return. I gave it to a friend—a multi-multi-millionaire—who had been extremely generous with my organization. Yes. I gave to him just as he had given to us so many times before. There was no reimbursement, no tax write-off. It was a gift just like he had given so many times to me.

I was transparent about the entire matter. He and his wife would stay for free. Any incidentals would be charged to my credit card. It was a literally a free stay at the lodge; he did have to pay for his transportation, but otherwise he would be living on my dime. I am certain that he naturally suspected there would be some pay-back; some overture for support. Nope. There was nothing planned. Weeks following the trip went by and as we continued our friendship he saw that our relationship had remarkable transparency. It earned great respect.

Clarify Your Agenda Beforehand

To the full extent possible, always attempt to let a person know your agenda ahead of time. Avoid the temptation to bait and switch. Donors, prospects and friends with whom I work know exactly what my job is and by inference, what I may be seeking from them. And, if they do not know, they will find out shortly. As a result I have made it an iron-clad habit of informing folks beforehand about exactly why I want to meet with them. Why have them sitting on the edge of their seats, defensive, anticipating that I am going to ask for money, when in fact the preponderance of our meetings are all about not asking for money? The difference in atmosphere, reception and demeanor is unbelievable.

Aha! Tip: Frank disclosure before meeting with prospects and donors will earn many friends and at the same time make it that much easier when it comes to talk about a gift because the same courtesy rule applies.

I consistently inform people of my intentions to discuss giving. That way if they are adamantly against the idea, they will usually let me know. This does not mean that a meeting does not take place; it means that a different meeting will occur, one which teases out their giving plans and enables me to better plan a solicitation meeting.

Relax

Whenever I have an engagement with an important prospect or donor, and I notice that I am becoming too anxious, I stop and ask myself, "What's the worst thing that could happen? After thinking about this for a few moments the answer inevitably surfaces: "nothing." I may not reach my fund or friend raising goal, but it is not the end of the world. In those situations where I am nervous about making a presentation I always remind myself that I can always terminate the conversation; ask for a follow-up meeting and then excuse myself. There is no reason to feel trapped.

Carefully Orchestrating Initial Contacts

The time honored adage is that you have only one chance to make a good first impression, and that is certainly the case when it comes to fundraising. As a result, special attention has to be devoted to making certain that initial contacts leave prospects and donors favorably disposed to a continuing relationship. These two ideas—first impressions are crucial to further development of a relationship, and act to ensure that the first contact is successful—are so fundamental, so rudimentary, that it seems almost laughable to repeat them here. However, in our busy-agenda-filled professional lives where multiple priorities compete repeatedly for our time and attention, inevitably it becomes easier to slack off on this highly important responsibility to form favorable impressions.

Few things bother me as much as knowing that I or a colleague has not completed requisite background research and meeting preparation sufficient to the task at hand. Many redeeming arguments are often offered to explain why we have not performed the appropriate due diligence. Nonetheless they are insufficient to overcome the fact that a client or prospect will not be cultivated at the highest level possible. And, if we look at this shortcoming from the other side, it is downright rude, a personal offense, that we did not care enough to invest suitable effort in respecting a new social contact.

Religiously Implement According to Plan

One final step remains in establishing the perfect architecture of a winning game plan. It is to execute these ideas consistently day-in-and-day-out. This is the slippery slope that dooms many people. These executives know what to do and how to go about it; but, they never get started, or they let themselves get bogged down in the process. This is precisely why and how Nike made such brand value with the phrase "Just do it." Good night, we love to talk about something but the execution never materializes.

Successful fundraising is all about "the doing of it." If executives would put more effort in getting started and less in procrastinating on things, the results would be overwhelming. Think of it…enough support flowing to our organizations that they actually have a reasonable probability of reaching their inspired visions. That image should be enough to encourage each of us to stay on task each and every day.

KEY AHA! POINTS

- Successful fundraisers generally follow a predictable, basic model that predisposes them for high performance.
- The key ingredients of a basic winning plan for fundraising by organizations include:
  - Undertaking sufficient preparation and planning
  - Setting the stage for positive results
  - Maintaining a positive image
  - Carefully orchestrating initial contacts
  - Conducting business with the highest levels of courtesy, integrity and enthusiasm.

- Follow the Rule of Two: make certain that appreciation is expressed both verbally and in writing.
  - Careful listening is an effective skill that facilitates fundraising and the key points in becoming a good listener include:
    - Listening to another person is equivalent to giving a gift. A receptive listener is a rare gem to discover.
    - Show respect by letting someone else talk first and focusing intently on what they have to say.
    - Look completely and continually into the other person's face in a polite and non-confrontation manner.
    - Concentrate on hearing what another person is telling you. It is one thing to listen and another to fully concentrate and process the other person's conversation.

- Remember that it takes two people to carry on a conversation.
- Engage the other person by guiding the discussion.
- If you want to dominate a conversation; don't.

Building Enduring Relationships

A gentle breeze occasionally swirled around our rustic wrought iron table overlooking the brilliant green foliage lining our river promenade. Meanwhile my deeply appreciated colleague caught up with me after a visit to her daughter's house back east. She had been gone almost a week and I had been crushed by handling her job and mine. All that misery would soon pass with her return. We were meeting for lunch to share details of what had transpired over the course of the past seven days. Truth be told, I was very happy to have her back so that we could address a couple of knotty problems that were creeping up on us.

But first, I wanted to hear about her trip….

After a review of the usual travel indignities that we all suffer these days, she turned to her family. The very first thing out of her mouth was a complaint about her beloved granddaughter—the first (and favorite) of her grandkids, "No sooner had we gotten into the house and dropped our luggage than Becky came running up to me and asked whether I had brought her anything." My good friend sat straight up and crossed her arms before exclaiming, "Imagine that!" "Apparently all I am good for is a present."

We laughed a little bit at the ferocity of her feelings and concluded that children will be children. But, I suspected that this was eating at her more than she was letting on. Certainly she was not the first grandparent to suddenly realize that her intended goal of showing love for her grandchildren via presents was being misconstrued. I let the matter lie rather than directing our conversation to the merits of giving, or not giving, to family members. Besides, it was time to get down to business.

Why is it that we can see the rudeness of our grandchildren or other family members so easily, and just as conveniently, overlook our transgressions with prospects and donors? Few people want to think that they are loved simply because they can give a good gift. That is tantamount to buying affection. Nonetheless, this is exactly what our prospects and donors often feel when all we can think about is a gift from them. We tend to imagine them as walking gift certificates. Such misguided attention is instrumental in chasing good prospects and donors away. Yes. Even prospects and donors need love too.

Figure 4-1 illustrates that successful fund raising hinges on the mindset with which we approach donors. In order to tip the scales in our favor, we need to accentuate building a relationship rather than getting a gift. The more that relationship-building is emphasized, the more that the scales will tilt toward receiving gifts that we seek. Success in fundraising hinges on those relationship behaviors that lead *naturally* to prospect and donor generosity.

Establish a Relationship First

How many colleagues can only think of counting a gift before anything else transpires? The answer is "too many." In the best-practice-is-to-go-out-and-bring-in-the-dough

Figure 4-1

Tipping the Scales in Your Favor

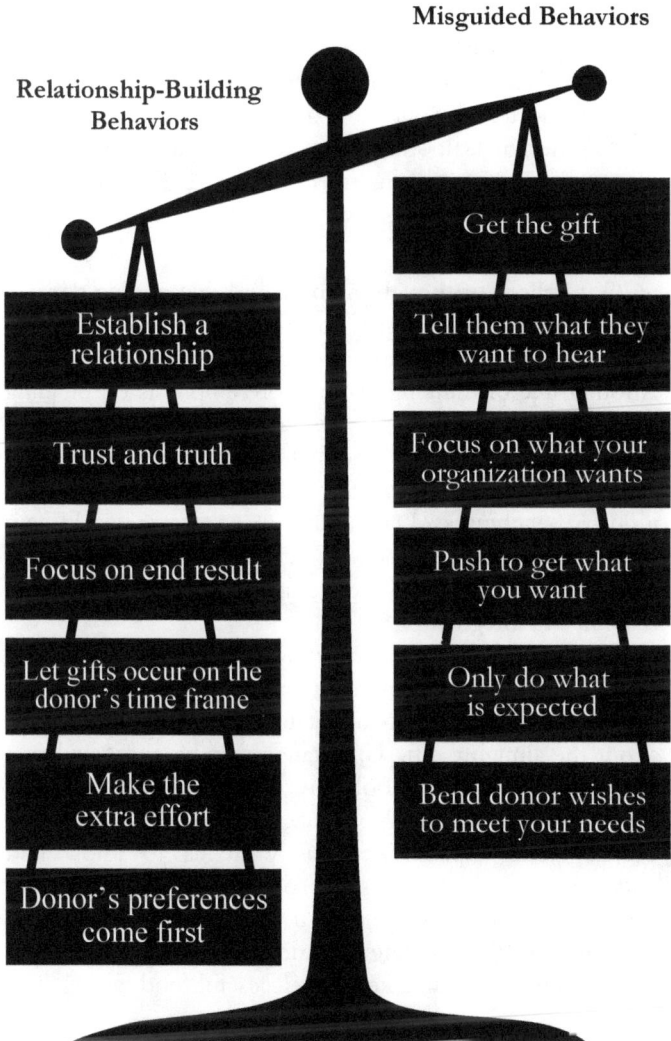

Misguided Behaviors

Relationship-Building Behaviors

Get the gift

Establish a relationship

Tell them what they want to hear

Trust and truth

Focus on what your organization wants

Focus on end result

Push to get what you want

Let gifts occur on the donor's time frame

Only do what is expected

Make the extra effort

Bend donor wishes to meet your needs

Donor's preferences come first

world there remains a little secret that too many are overlooking. Challenging people to make a sale may be acceptable in business; but making people capitulate to a donation is not a winning long-run strategy.[7] Successful fund raising *is all about* relationships.

Aha! Tip: The goal of successful friend and fund raising is not to score by bringing in a gift in the shortest amount of time. Any executive worth her/his salt should know, and practice, the art of building enduring relationships before seeking a major donation.

One school of thought admonishes that getting a gift is our first-and-foremost professional responsibility. Everything else becomes a secondary consideration. Another line of thinking places more emphasis on building long-run relationships. In truth, enlightened fund raising is not a new idea. But, it is one that can easily be forgotten in a world driven to demonstrate short-run progress against industry benchmarks. Let us not forget that it is not difficult to measure the number of dollars raised, but it is exceedingly difficult to create a deeply rich metric of relationship integrity.

Almost nothing in philanthropy is as shallow as a person who does not understand that common decency requires working with donors to understand *them* before thinking about the almighty gift. This stance may be construed as a bit too much of old school fundraising, but guess what? It simply works. Period. People *do* want to be treated with decency and respect. They *do* want us to know and understand them, have insights on what drives them, and appreciate what they value even if we may disagree.

Consequently, building enduring relationships is one of the big two unassailable keys to successful fund raising. The other key is the ability to articulate and follow a compelling mission and/or vision that excites donors. Which is number one and which is number two? Priority probably does not matter. These are the two indispensable cornerstones behind rethinking successful fund and friend raising.

AHA! CASE INSIGHT

A classic example of the short-sightedness of focusing first on fund raising dates back to a visit I made to a distinguished businessman. The first words I heard about him were glowing. No one talked about his impressive wealth, although he was wildly successful with multiple houses and ranches. All who had met him shared a common sentiment that this was one of the most genuinely loveable people on the face of this earth. "You just feel good when you are around him." "He makes you feel like you are the center of attention." These were only a few of the expressed opinions that friends and colleagues divulged to me. I made a note that I had to meet him. And I made a second note to try more diligently to follow in his footsteps; to make others the center of attention and to make others feel special for my presence. If it worked for him, why couldn't it work for me?

Some weeks later I asked a colleague to accompany me on an initial visit with this special person. We flew for an hour-plus and landed in the big city at morning rush hour. He had reserved a car, but I suggested that we take a taxi to the downtown business district given all of the traffic. He agreed and we hoped in the cab. Seven minutes later on the freeway our cab driver made a very quick lane change to avoid cars stopped in front of him. The lady riding our tail did not see it coming and she ran smack into the car in front of her. As we pulled away I looked back and said to my colleague that had we taken the time to secure a rental car we would now be stuck in the massive traffic jam that was forming behind us. The trip would possibly have been ruined.

In no time at all we pulled up to this city's tallest skyscraper and made our way to a top floor. Our appointment greeted us like long lost friends. "Smitty," he said to me, "how are you doing?" Now...that is exactly how I want our donors, our friends, to greet me.

What infectious good cheer he radiated. The feeling was akin to going home to grandmother's for the holidays and walking in and sitting down at her kitchen table as she pulled a fresh-baked sheet of your favorite cookies out of the oven. He made me feel like we had known each other for years and we were now just catching up a bit on recent events. He had performed some prior surveillance sufficient to know just enough critical background details that we could converse in a comfortable, informed way. This signaled that he was genuinely interested in me; I was not just another superficial acquaintance to be mollified before he returned to bigger issues this day.

The conversation bantered back-and-forth about exciting things that were happening. He made certain that everyone participated equally in the conversation; no one dominated. I enjoyed this aspect as it gave me time to relax, sit back and take a measure of the man in the same manner as he was sitting across from me and sizing me up.

Suddenly without warning this prominent businessman said to me, "Well I haven't given you any money in a long time, how about me writing a check for $100,000?" For half of a second I almost did not know what to say. Then the purpose of this meeting came flooding back.

"Oh, I appreciate your kind offer but I did not come here to ask you for money."

He sat there with a puzzled look for a moment.

I stole a glance at my colleague. He looked like I had belched in his face. I could see the gears going in his brain, "What are you, stupid? The guy just offered you $100,000."

Our friend came back a second time. "Oh certainly you can use $100,000 for something can't you?"

"No, when I asked to meet you I believe I said I was just coming over to meet you. I didn't say I was coming to make a proposal. We can talk about money some other time."

My refusal to be distracted from the purpose of our meeting buffaloed him for a second; he paused a bit, and then we launched back into a free-wheeling discussion about his grandsons who are accomplished athletes on the road to being recruited by many colleges and universities. It was a great half-hour conversation that flourished because we focused first and foremost on getting to know each other.

Eventually it was time to go. We had overstayed our visit by about fifteen minutes and I was concerned that we had strayed from our schedule and purpose. With hearty handshakes, hugs and remembrances we left his office and made our way to the elevator. I had already educated my colleague about never, ever, rehashing or reacting to a meeting on the same premises. Our debriefing, even a celebration, could wait until we were in the taxi.

With a resonant "bling," the elevator door popped open and we stepped aside as a smartly dressed, young woman wearing the name tag of a local nonprofit organization stepped out. We entered the elevator and after the doors closed I said to my colleague, "Well, there goes the competition." We both chortled and waited patiently to reach ground level, hopped into the taxi and were on our way back home.

Over the course of the next two hours at the airport and in the air as we flew back, ideas bounced back and forth about the next step. At the top of the storyboard was what program, project or initiative we could build a proposal around to present to my new friend. A nice six-figure gift could be used in so many ways; but, we wanted to tailor the request to his specific interests. Like a ping pong ball suggestions floated back and forth as we rode the friendly skies toward home. Our discussion continued hot and heavy regarding options once we landed.

Surprisingly there was still enough time that afternoon to drop by the office and get caught up on phone calls, emails, and crises. It is funny how much falls apart in the course of a day. With an "uummmppphhh" I flopped into my chair and thought to myself that these trips get harder every day. After only three seconds of peaceful bliss, the chief financial officer of our foundation knocked on my door and came in to inform me that the businessman we had just visited wired $200,000. Apparently the money was sent while we were still in the air winging our way home.

I should have known. People of unusual character tend to do things with a flair that leaves the rest of us running to catch up. He made his point; but I also had been rewarded for sticking to principle. Build a relationship first.

Trust and Truth

It is a joy to behold when you are able to build a solid bond of trust with donors, clients and friends. Unfortunately, there are few ways to build trust except over time and from repeated interactions that allow others to gain insights into how you think, behave and make decisions. I tend to lump trust with truth because looking back on hundreds of rock-solid relationships always telling the truth inevitably led to trust. I will admit that there were times when I squirmed in my seat because the news I was about to deliver was not necessarily what my friend wanted to hear. But I always have gotten to the guts of the matter while trying to be impartial in my presentation. Objectivity seems to make telling the difficult truth that much easier.

AHA! CASE INSIGHT

My assistant came into my office and as she took a seat she gently closed the door. That was a bad sign. Either she had very bad news to tell me, or she did not want what she had to say to leak out—perhaps it was both. I pulled my hand off the mouse and leaned back, sucking up a huge measure of oxygen expecting to hear something that I did not want to hear. She sat erect waiting for me to acknowledge that I was ready to fully concentrate on what she had to say.

"Wwwweeelll?"

"We just endured another visit by Donor X," she retorted very sharply. After five years of working with my superb assistant I knew enough not to open my mouth. She was just getting started.

"He spent the last five minutes beating up our receptionist while using the foulest language imaginable. In fact he...." I tuned out my beloved assistant's detail laden diatribe about this donor who had a nasty habit of unloading on staff about the most unimportant matters. This was not the first time that a staff member had shared with others about his peculiar traits. But, this was the first time anyone had brought one of their complaints directly to me, well sort of directly, via my assistant.

She continued to harangue him and to document an increasing line on verbal abuse that was downright intolerable. While she flailed away I listened intently with my eyes focused on her. Meanwhile I was trying to put it all together. With community members and people in executive positions he was the most decent, cordial and ethical paragon of virtue that walked this planet. Most likened him to a cuddly puppy dog that cried for love and attention. Even the most callous wanted to engage him in conversation. I had witnessed this phenomenon at several meetings/events. He attracted a huge entourage of groupies who would not leave him alone no matter where he wandered in a reception.

My assistant began to sum up her position. In my mind I tried to remember how much this venerable gentleman had given to my institution. Was it $700,000? No, he had given over $1.2 million and he had informed us about an enormous planned gift of $4 million. Oh boy.

"So you see, we cannot tolerate this anymore." She stopped.

I waited.

"And???" I queried.

"Oh nothing more, I just feel that…"

Before she could reload and repeat herself I nipped it in the bud, "What he is doing is patently disrespectable and an insult to all our staff.' Please make a luncheon appointment with him and I will put a stop to his offending behavior."

She was caught off guard a bit by my reaction. Obviously she was thinking that she would have to defend the idea of addressing this lout because of the generous gifts he had made. "Do you have a day in mind…?" The wheels were in motion.

One week later I took my seat across from this donor. He had already made his promenade through our exclusive private club. A hand wave here and a sweet smile there; he made the rounds among the rich and influential of his boyhood home.

We went through the usual run of show for lunch. Casual humor about my boss' latest faux pas and clever insights on local business ventures consumed our preliminary soup time as well as half of the time whacking our way through hefty salad entrees. Finally, he stopped short and said, "But you didn't want to meet with me about these frivolities, what is really on your mind?

Ah, yes, the ever subliminally perceptible, rigorously analytic side of him popped out. It was always lurking there beneath the surface, just like his propensity to bash the hired help.

"Well X," as I used his first name, "I have a bit of a problem. You see…." I went on to thank him for his generous giving and for his leadership of our initiatives. But, I needed to level with him about how he treated my staff even if it meant that we would lose a friend. I aimed squarely for the middle of his forehead and shot a huge caliber bullet of truth right at him.

He didn't flinch, but he did shake his head slightly to the right while looking down at his plate and then gently raised his eyes to stare directly in mine. "Jolly good for you. You are right. I have treated your staff like peons and abused them horribly. I know I have a problem, and I work to keep it under control. I will do my best to stop.

"No," I responded. "That is not good enough. Somewhat-stopping is not an option. These are great people. They deserve to be treated with dignity. It has to stop."

Again he shook his head slightly and stared me in the eyes.

"You have my word."

Two months later he dropped by our offices and left a little envelope for me. Our receptionist mentioned how cordially he treated her. She was swept up in his charm. I was very happy to receive this report from my assistant as she handed me an envelope.

She paused without turning to go.

"Yes," I queried?

"Oh, nothing. It thought you would want to open the envelope."

Which I did. Inside was a donation for $50,000. Not quite on par with previous gifts, it was more of a handshake to say "you were right" and to confirm that he was still an enduring friend. Truth led to trust and confirmation that going forward I could count on him to behave as genteelly toward my staff as he did to his long-time cronies at our private club. From that moment forward we enjoyed a special friendship that was much richer due to the full bouquet of truth and trust that permeated our relationship.

Focus on the End Result not on a Want

Is there any better way to undermine an enduring relationship than to obsessively keep focusing on what you want? Self-centered people inevitably just do not get it. They can only think of what is on their agenda rather than taking a genuine interest in or having compassion for another person. This may be the most egregious error that fundraisers routinely commit without recognizing the error of their ways. We often become so goal-driven that we lose sight of what we are actually doing. Literature on leadership effectiveness and best management practices certainly underscores the sacrosanct imperative of identifying a goal and methodically pursuing it to final accomplishment.[8-9] This sort of blind pursuit inevitably creates a monster; the tyranny of a goal overrides the sensibility of decent human interactions.

Even deeply cemented friendships can begin to unravel when single-minded goal obsession displaces valued collegiality. Prospects and donors are incredibly sensitive to real intentions and from the moment of that first introduction, they suspect that your friendly demeanor is nothing but a façade or a false front hiding real intentions. Consequently it takes a heroic effort to build a strong relationship with donors that is not somehow tinged with a patina of greed; lust for a donation that helps *you* meet *your* goal and conveniently depreciates the human connection.

Many of my colleagues have excitedly shared their proposed next step in cultivating a major donor. I patiently listen as they sketch out the details of their brilliant strategy. They have invested numerous meetings in getting to know donors in a superficial way, and thus feel that they can waltz in at a time that is convenient to them and make a big "ask." It is all about getting another financial commitment that is essential to the mini-campaign being waged by their unit. Seldom, if ever, do I also first hear their thoughts about how a donor or prospect is doing…what is going on their lives; how they have overcome a personal struggle; how sensitive they are to long-run economic forecasts; whether a solicitation proposal at this point is well-timed given events in their lives; or similar sentiments about the well-being of a supposed friend.

Aha! Tip: We are obsessed with what we want rather than being obsessed with the higher end result which is the donor as a friend and ardent supporter.

Let me be very frank in admitting that during my formative years I too committed these sorts of blunders. I erroneously focused on the almighty dollar-oriented goal to the exclusion of dwelling on what is right or noble. How can a young professional not succumb to these sorts of pressures? Once you have tasted the victory of landing a large gift and become swept up in the accolades generously showered upon you, it is very difficult to behave otherwise. The positive reinforcement for a job well done feels great. In this harshly objective world, there are too few moments of appreciation, insufficient praise for doing a good job. It is difficult to argue against the hard reality of those numbers—six- and seven-figure gifts that have everyone proclaiming your stature as genius, and launch toward wunderkind status.

But, this is not the way to become effective in fundraising over the long haul.

> **Aha! Tip:** Demonstrable long-run success in fund raising means that you are more interested in the relationships you build with people and particularly the relationships you build with people that support your program.

Anyone can raise a lot of money over the short run by not investing in the end (the relationship) and focusing instead on the want (the money). After all, building a relationship takes lots of time, hard work, effort and genuine personal investment. It is far easier to set donors and prospects up for a quick ask, and then move along to the next target once you have discovered whether or not they will support your particular want. I think the profession can do much better than this; it should be about relationships not handouts.

In order to prevent succumbing to a compulsive spotlight on getting a gift to the exclusion of building a long-term relationship, it helps to frame fundraising in terms of what assets are needed to get the job done rather than in terms of a specific want.

AHA! CASE INSIGHT

I was trying to raise funds to retain a former female astronaut on our staff. Once I heard about this opportunity I was gung-ho to get out there and bring in the funding essential to attract her to our institution.

As I devised a strategy to raise the funds sufficient to cover the astronaut's expense, and well before I met her, a video clip of her speaking at a public forum was forwarded to me for review. I was blown away by the sincerity of this person about better educating children. It was hard to imagine a more decent, intelligent, compassionate, dedicated and child-supportive person. A few days later I met her in person; here was someone whose heart was in the right place. She embodied the drive and aspiration that we want to instill in all young people. The sky is the limit if you adequately prepare yourself with a good education, concentrate on the task at hand, work hard, and believe in yourself.

Predictably my thinking turned toward the astronaut as a role model for young girls and boys. She embodied the means for children to envision what is possible in life career-wise, and the message for them to go after that dream without any pre-conceived thoughts about personal constraints. This became the concept that I shared with folks who I thought would support the astronaut in her endeavors at my institution. To help them better envision what we had already seen as her invaluable contribution to children in our state, I offered up the following challenge.

First, envision an elementary school child watching the astronaut on T.V. as she talks about her space flight, floating in the space capsule, staring down on planet earth, conducting scientific investigations.

The child exclaims to her/his parent, "I want to do that."

Second, because we have retained the astronaut on our staff, she visits the elementary school where this child attends. The child hangs on the astronaut's every word and imagines that she/he is the astronaut floating about in the spaceship, reading the stars and performing important research studies.

That evening the child exclaims to his/her parent, "I can do that."

Third, this elementary student eventually graduates from high school and studies science, technology, engineering or math.

As the now grown child goes out the door to college to follow in the astronaut's footsteps, she/he says, "I will do that."

How much more powerful is a message to a friend than this? We are essentially saying, "We need your help in acquiring resources to bring a former astronaut on staff. This person will help children move their level of thinking from 'I want to do that' to 'I can do that;' and, ultimately, to 'I will do that' as far career ambitions are concerned." Shifting the emphasis from "we want [funds]" to "would you help support" makes all the difference in the world as far as message is concerned. It involves the donor friend in a massively important undertaking with hugely far-reaching implications.

As the preceding illustration conveys, a friend opens opportunities to other friends. In contrast, a casual acquaintance asks other non-friends for money. This is another way of viewing the shift from "want" to talking about an end result. Donors still recognized that the end result is to round up funds to support the former astronaut. But they also read this as a unique opportunity that they could be involved in as far as support is concerned. The nuance is not minuscule, it is commanding. It is the sort of distinction that leads to long-term relationship building with friends as opposed to just soliciting funds from the next prospect on a list.

Pushing Seldom Builds Long-term Relationships

Do not push donors if you want to build enduring long-term relationships. The operative word here is "long-term." Virtually every organization I have worked with or interacted has gone about business as though they would last forever. Most entities do enjoy the largesse of time…more so than the relationship that executives make with people of influence and means that they cultivate. Nonetheless, executives have to be ever-vigilant that they do not sacrifice the goal of maintaining a relationship because they have been too eager to push a donor for money.

Some time ago when I chaired the board of a state's largest home health, durable equipment and hospice agency I had my first opportunity to join a colleague as we met with a major donor of substantial means. His family had given munificently over the years, but disappointingly at a modest six-figure level. We knew that his financial prospects were extremely upbeat since he had recently sold a multi-state enterprise. His net worth was probably in the $30-50 million range. I was looking forward to meeting him and hearing his story about how the empire had grown. It had to be an impressive undertaking since most of the very successful outlets were located in relatively small, rural towns. My colleague confided that actually there was no proposal to present; this was merely a meet-and-greet on my behalf and a stewardship call on his part.

We joined the donor for lunch at a reasonable restaurant. After initial pleasantries, a quick walk through the menu and completely different orders by three people that covered almost every spectrum of the food continuum, we briefly exchanged backgrounds and settled into the donor's recitation of phases he went through to build a tidy empire. He shared some of the creative thinking on his part, and strategic blunders by competitors, that spoke volumes about business acumen. Included were several hilarious scenarios and amid one of these hysterical vignettes, our food arrived.

The interruption offered just enough of a break for my colleague to suddenly switch gears in the conversation. He decided to drill down into our donor's thinking about a generous contribution to a new mini-campaign surrounding our headquarters. Frankly, I about choked on my BLT. This meeting was NOT supposed to be about a gift proposal. Our donor gave a sharp retort that essentially said, "I have given plenty to your organization." I managed to interject a comment about how much we DID appreciate the donor's gifts.

In the end it was picture-perfect example of how little good can be achieved when a donor is pushed. That little frivolous moment of excess by my colleague halted cultivation of this donor for a four-year period. Think twice, no, think three times before ever trying to push a donor for anything.

Make the Extra Effort

Cultivation and solicitation of personal gifts thrive when every effort is made to go the extra mile. I often come close to breaking my hand by patting myself on the back for working so hard to cultivate a donor. And then I look around me and I see some colleague going that extra distance, delivering beyond-exceptional care to a donor; I pause to remember that I am virtually an amateur compared to the noble efforts some of my colleagues put forward. Donors recognize, appreciate and resonate with these fine touches. A few take advantage of such good intentions. They become spoiled and expect royal treatment above and beyond the call of duty. Most, however, deepen their friendship and look for ways to pay back the kindness.

AHA! CASE INSIGHT

I received word that a very successful entrepreneur had died. This kindly friend, who was always prepared to add a jovial touch of humor in even the most dismal of circumstances, would never share special moments with me again. My spirit plummeted and my heart sank. What an abysmal day it would be until we closed shop.

As if the pronouncement somehow made up for the loss, the person on the other end of the phone gleefully informed me that the entrepreneur left a $1 million endowment to my department. I guess that was supposed to make up for losing one of the most genuinely compassionate people I have ever known. Honestly, I did not even respond back. A ringing silence filled the phone. My caller repeated, "Did you hear that he left $1 million to your department?" "Yeah; great," I spouted back. "Thanks for the call." This was just what I didn't need. I was $1 million richer and had lost a truly exceptional friend.

Fast forward one month. My boss called to inform me that within the next three months we would honor this gentleman's family, his surviving son and relatives, at a dinner to recognize his accomplishments and generosity. "That could be a sticky one," I thought because I had heard that the son was contesting the final will and testament. In his next breath my boss asked me when we could hold the dinner. I told him that my calendar would be made completely empty *except* for April 3-5. On those days I would be out of state on an accreditation visit. "Please do not schedule it for those days because I cannot change my schedule."

A few weeks later I was going through my mail when I can upon a very fancy invitation addressed to me. I opened the expensive envelope and discovered a very formal and stylish announcement of a dinner the night of April 4 to honor my deceased friend and family. Go figure. I guess it was too much trouble to avoid a day when I would be out-of-town. It was obvious that I could not now argue to change the event date; I also could not change the accreditation review dates. However, I really needed to be at that dinner. I was honor-bound. It was time to shift into creative-thinking mode.

Although I subjected my assistant to a massive attention-to-detail scheduling effort, we finally made arrangements to fly 800 miles back on the evening of April 4 to my hometown from where the accreditation review was taking place. After dashing out on the review team I drove like a fiend to the local airport and then caught a flight just in time to arrive one hour before the celebratory dinner was scheduled. A colleague picked me up at the airport and whisked me to the dinner. At 6:00 a.m. the next morning a flight would take me back to the accreditation review.

My boss had arranged for me to sit next to the donor's son. This was the payoff for working the unthinkable. As the crowd of 125 people sat down in their places I finally had the time to express my condolences and to further share what his father had meant to me as a friend. I think I was getting through, but there remained a bit of distance, a smidgen of skepticism in his eyes, suggesting that he thought my allegiance probably had everything to do with the seven-figure gift. I passed the rolls as my boss stepped to the podium to say a few kind words and to encourage us to begin our meal.

The son casually asked how my day had gone. I had nothing to hide so I told him how amazing it was to be two states away at an accreditation visit; to put in a full day of meetings; and then to be able to join him for dinner tonight after a bit of hasty travel. If everything went according to plan I would be back on-site, two states away, by 8:30 a.m.

He was flabbergasted, truly astounded, that I would go to all that effort.

Words cannot adequately convey the heart-felt appreciation that commandeered his eyes and voice. He shared this little story effusively with every member at our table and then he got up out of his chair and went over to my boss to deliver his impression of my going that extra mile to be present. As I watched him speak expressively with his hands and animated features I intuitively knew that a new, stronger relationship had been forged. Building on the base his father had hewn, this would continue to be an enduring family relationship equivalent to the fine character and legacy of a stellar patriarch.

And, yes; everything fell into place on my travel the next morning. Almost no one knew that I spent the night in my own bed. It had been a deeply sweet sleep.

A Donor's Preferences Come First

Truly lasting relationships are built with donors by following a policy of the customer comes first. There are at least two ways to view this statement. On the one hand I am reminded of a colleague who patently insisted that I should never use business terms like "sales," "customers," or "marketing" in philanthropic work because (somehow) fundraising does not lower itself to such blasé concepts. On the other hand, this policy of the customer coming first possesses a purity, and reality, that cannot be denied. A donor's preferences should come first. It is never about what we want; it is always about what donors want to achieve with their gift.

It is as plain and straightforward as that. Try as we might, the inherent logic and validity of donors' preferences rule (whether that agrees with our personal biases or not). Granted, what the donor wants as far as allocation and impact of a gift, may not be exactly what we are hoping for. However, our concerns are secondary to making certain that a donor's gift supports exactly what a donor intended. Let's look at a case in point.

AHA! CASE INSIGHT

My institution had been cultivating a very wealthy individual for years. He was a captain of economic development; a land developer who had won accolades for his stylish, trendy and attractive modest business parks. He did not merely arrive at that reputation by erecting a few buildings. He had a legacy of business parks spread over and across our community. And, he had been very generous to a few organizations. Consequently every nonprofit organization with a good cause wanted to get on his calendar. I had a number of business acquaintances who felt this developer and I shared a common interest in the outdoors and wild country. Eventually one shared interest brought this seasoned veteran and me together for a quick lunch.

Intensity. That was the first characteristic that made an impression on me as I listened to this new acquaintance. He led off with a brief inventory of his business parks. It was a very long inventory, but I enjoyed watching him and his craggy features as they punctuated this point and that. He knew hard work both indoors and out. Given his resume and his single-minded attention to detail, he had built an empire where others were merely bit-players. This was not someone to be taken lightly. He continued with his description of his latest building initiative when the waitperson brought over our drinks. I was poised for the next moment because his friend who joined us for this lunch had filled me in on the gentleman's proclivities.

My guest was well-known for occupying the same table at lunch time almost every day of the week. Fridays he might be absent if it was bird season because he would be out in the field with his beloved hunting dog. By the same token, he had his "usual" meal every day, a small steak, unless fresh halibut was on the menu. True to form, he placed his order and then we began regaling one another with tales from outdoor adventures. It was respect at first sight and from that moment forward he and I had both discovered a new best friend. Each of us reveled in the other's tales about outdoor craft and living a big full life among wilderness and wild creatures.

Thus the friendship matured over the next few years. He feigned interest in making a large gift, but my work was not to cultivate him. Another staff member had that firmly in command. I was able to enjoy the privilege of purely knowing him, his family, his business and his dog. I took this responsibility very seriously and made every attempt to take our relationship to the highest honorable level.

Eventually my friend began making noises about contributing to our organization. He would drop a hint or two in a conversation, nothing much more than a veiled allusion. I did not react to these mini-overtures. If he wanted to seriously talk about a gift I was quite willing to do so, but I did not want to play the game of him thinking that I would sacrifice our relationship for a buck. If and when he was ready I was certain that I would know about because he was that kind of person. All cards were laid on the table or you did not play the game at all.

A few days later my colleague who was cultivating him for a gift proudly announced that the gentlemen in question had told her that he would be making a seven-figure gift to Program A. From what I could tell she was rubbing the announcement in my face. I had to admit that my new donor friend had not consulted me or bothered to share any plans, but that did not truly matter as far as I was concerned. More power to my colleague. We both worked for the same organization so it was not a contest in my mind. Certainly I would have suggested Program B where the impact was that much more promising, but in the final analysis it did not matter. Support was needed for both meritorious causes.

I'll confess that as I turned from my conversation with my colleague, the thought that my donor friend did not first share his thinking with me stung a bit. I began to question whether our friendship was all in my mind. Regardless, I enjoyed his camaraderie and counsel; that was friendship enough from my perspective. I continued out the door and went home for the day, my mind spinning about other matters more weighty than whether I had been skunked by my ambitious contemporary.

Several hours later as darkness filled our streets the phone rang at home. I managed to grab the phone by the fourth ring and prepared to lambast another solicitor. Surprise; surprise. At the other end was my faithful friend. He called to say that he had decided to make a seven-figure gift, but he wanted to know where I would assign the gift. He explicitly trusted my judgment and that would be that. Before I could say a word he slipped in that my contemporary was recommending Project A. He, however, was thinking that Project B might be a better fit with a higher need.

In all honesty I paused for about ten seconds. For once I let my brain do the thinking before my mouth began talking. Over a few nanoseconds I rehearsed what I was about to say. It seemed correct but I hesitated knowing that I was about to say one thing that my brain commanded when my heart meant another.

"My friend," I began, "thank you for asking me my opinion. There is no doubt that Project A suggested by my colleague is one of our organization's leading initiatives." I proceeded to define the wonderful aspects of Project A and the impressive outcomes that would arise due to his seven-figure gift. This support would give Project A resources that could launch it on a path to national fame. I speculated about all of the constituents, primarily children, who would be touched by this initiative. I asked him to think with me to the long-run one-hundred years from now and how people might benefit from Program A's presence. It was a very luminous image.

Then I shifted back to Project B. I scrutinized Project B on the exact same dimensions as I did for Project A. Project B simply glowed on some dimensions and Project A stole the show on others. It was a very honest appraisal and certainly communicated that either option was a praiseworthy investment.

I stopped for a couple of seconds to gather my breath, hesitated while gulping another breath and then delivered the verdict. I told him that I thought he was more interested in Project A and would be happier supporting Project A. He muffled a little cough and then began drilling down into me about Project B. He knew it was one of my favorite initiatives. He firmly said that he thought he would rather choose Project B. He repeated all of the beneficial points I had made.

I was astounded. He would rather invest seven-figures in what made me happy than what made him happy. How much of a testament does one need before it smacks you on the side of the head that you have been blessed with a truly remarkable friend? I could not accept his generosity and I told him point blank to donate the money to Project A because it was what his life stood for and what he wanted to leave as a signature give-forward. He mumbled a few protestations and then queried, "Are you certain?" "Yes," I replied, "Very certain that Project A is the right choice for you." "Alright," he said," I will inform your colleague."

As much as I wanted Project B to receive those funds, all these years later I remain convinced that the correct choice was made. He selected the project that was closest to his heart and soul. Any other selection was out of the question.

A donor's preference rules. Period. That is how you build and maintain enduring relationships.

KEY AHA! POINTS

- The goal of successful fundraising is to build enduring relationships first and then attend to informing a prospect about your organization's compelling mission. Solicitation of a donation comes next.

- Reinforce trust by always telling the truth. Once a person trusts you then conduct business as though both trust and truth are of utmost importance.

- Be obsessed with what you want will only be to the detriment of the higher end result which is the donor as a friend and ardent supporter.

- Demonstrable long-run success in fund raising means that you are most interested in the relationships you build with people.

- Pushing seldom results in speeding up the donation of a gift.

- Cultivation and solicitation of personal gifts thrive when every effort is made to go the extra mile.

- Donor preferences always come first. If they don't, then do not be surprised if a donor walks away.

Imaginative Thinking

Ingenuity.
Imagination.
Creativity.

There is positively no substitute for thinking cleverly when it comes to friend and fund raising. Unfortunately most executives are so busy dotting their "i's" and crossing their "t's" that they never have quality time to move forward in a truly inspired way. It doesn't have to be this way. Perhaps there are no cure-all answers that will free executives from the mind-numbing minutiae that they are saddled with. But, a number of suggestions are fortunately available for thinking more creatively in the fundraising arena. The first lesson begins with a case study that illustrates how to think more creatively.

AHA! CASE INSIGHT

This was one luncheon that I had really been looking forward to; now if I could just remember that I had a full afternoon when I ordered my meal. Endless meetings would go very late into the day. Making the right decision on what to eat was so essential because a willowy high-end salad would only leave me desperate for fat-laced calories three hours later. I mentally ran down the possibilities when pulling open a marvelous mahogany entrance door to our private club where all the so important movers and shakers meet. A heavy sigh escaped as I fought back dark thoughts about impression management and the need to play these games. But…it is what it is.

Our ever alert and buoyant hostess greeted me with a warm "Good day Dr. Smith; your party is already here. Please follow me." She spun while grabbing a leather-encased menu and we began our courtly promenade down the center of the dining room. "Hey everyone…it's me," I thought as we pranced toward a choice table overlooking the green-gray flowing river. From years of practice I discreetly scanned the expansive open room which was flooded with soft yellow light, giving a nod here, a little wave there, a soft "Hello" to a person I really admired, and a wink to a partner in crime.

Ahhh. Our little gathering is approaching. My colleague, ever radiant with her beguiling smile, is deep in a rapid-fire conversation with our prospects, but she is on the ball enough to acknowledge my approach with a little nod of her head and a quick flit of her eyes. I'll never be as good at these charades as she is because she really does love all of this theater.

Our guests have enormous wealth. Late forty-something, he is in one of the leading legal practices and she is the daughter of one of the wealthiest couples in the state. It is definitely good to be them. She has a past, uninspired, affiliation with my organization.

Our meeting today is benign. There is no goal except to meet and greet. They have never made a contribution to the hallowed halls of my employer, but this tete-a-tete could be the launch point for building a fruitful relationship. We need to be patient, not get greedy, and let these nefarious matters take their due course. Frankly I love these sessions of getting to know interesting people, sharing a bit about the mesmerizing mission of our organization, and listening to life stories of two people who seemingly have it made.

After proper introductions by my extremely capable colleague, we order up and settle back to share a bit about ourselves. Everything is tracking perfectly. Best of all inspired genius made me order the low-cal plate, essentially a cheap ground beef patty with cottage cheese for volume and a fruit cup for the constitution. Brilliant under the circumstances.

As our conversation rallies back-and-forth around the table, our female guest lays it right out there before I realize what is happening. "We would like to make a $2,500 donation." With that brief prelude, she pulls out a previously prepared check.

All I can think to myself is, "Whooppppeee!" This is fantastic. I really mean it. To this point we have received nothing from them. Absolutely nothing has ever been received from this cornerstone family of our community. Our foot is in the proverbial front door. My colleague jumps in with perfect timing—profuse expressions of appreciation and sincere overtones of how this gift will positively affect the lives of so many. She prattles on with an appropriate injected "Thank you so much" while I add, "This means a great deal to our program."

In truth my mind is elsewhere at this moment as my colleague goes over the details. I am already trying to figure out how to make this gift stretch farther and give us an opportunity to demonstrate to these kind folks how much we really do treasure this gift. It is also essential to carefully determine how we will use it to leverage other gifts in the future. The key is having enough opportunities to show these donors their impact and to validate that they have received a superior return on their investment of $2,500.

Before I know it, we have whisked through dessert and gotten up to leave. It has been a long lunch; much too long given the smattering of few patrons left chewing the fat. Time to get back to the office and to think this over.

As I drive down the same old path I travel several times a week, I examine the facts. Here is a family of gigantic wealth that has been almost estranged from my institution. This is the first peace offering and an opportunity that should not be wasted. Most executives involved in fundraising would happily report the gift, add it to their monthly tally, and set about preparing the paperwork to document the gift, steward the donors with appreciation, and make the deposit. I do not want to react like a typical bureaucrat. This is a momentous occasion; we need to leverage this like pros.

I lean all the way back in my office chair thinking about the tried, traditional, and trite ways that this opportunity is normally managed. An idea began to sprout in my mind. To this point we have dutifully followed the fundraising guide chapter-by-chapter, paragraph-by-paragraph and letter-by-letter. Now it is time to think out of the box. Ninety-nine percent of all other people would be thinking about the next step. They would focus on months forward when they will arrange another lunch with these donors to begin hinting about another gift; or, they would speculate about various program staff they might introduce them to in order to build the relationship. All of these are absolutely great strategies and worthy of merit in the fundraising hall of fame. But something extraordinary is needed this time.

The vast majority of executives would be concentrating on the next step. I reversed this idea. What would happen if I took the next step? What could I do to move this along more quickly in order to accelerate the relationship and future prospects? Without further hesitation I picked up the phone and dialed my colleague because I think I knew exactly what to do to truly make this $2,500 gift into a milestone beginning.

Before returning to the $2,500 gift and how it was enhanced to accelerate donor development, it is essential to first explore the idea of ingenious thinking.

Reversing the Algorithm

If I had to point to only one idea that makes the most difference in successful friend and fund raising, it would be the notion of reversing the algorithm. In order to inject a good measure of ingenuity into philanthropy, it is very productive to take a contrarian perspective. Consider how a problem is normally addressed, and then turn that approach completely around to gain impressive new insight into different strategies.

For example, I serve on a board of directors of an organization that annually holds a fund raising dinner from its donors. As I joined the board planning began for the next dinner. Several board members noted that attendance had fallen off, although revenues held steady. A couple of board representatives suggested that we needed to bring in new prospects and this dinner would be a good introduction. Yet, on the face of it, these goals—raise funds; bring in new prospects—seemed to be at cross-purposes.

Aha! Tip: Is there any better way to chase off prospects than at your first meeting press them for a contribution when they do not even know what compelling mission your organization fulfills?

Reverse the algorithm. If the algorithm is having an annual dinner, then the algorithm reversed is to consider providing a breakfast or lunch…anything but another dinner. In our discussion we decided that we would only have a reception with heavy hors d'oeuvres. If the algorithm is pressing long-time patrons to make a donation, then the algorithm reversed is to consider not making a request for a contribution at the event. In our deliberations we settled on informing our long-time friends about the return on investment, the outcomes, we had attained through their generous gifts. In retrospect we had never properly informed them about the results that their dollars produced. And, we decided to follow-up with a phone-call to every attendee within two weeks after the reception was completed.

If the algorithm is holding an annual dinner on a Saturday with a 2 hour-long program then reverse the algorithm. As we drilled more deeply into comments shared by donors after the last two dinners, we concluded that our friends thought these events went too long. The algorithm reversed was to hold a reception for 45 minutes; period. We planned accordingly and stuck to a rigorous "run-of-show" that finished on time. The algorithm reversed was moving the event to a late Sunday afternoon to avoid that lethargy that accompanies Friday evenings and to avoid the action-packed Saturday night events. Finally, if the algorithm has traditionally been to invite only donors, then the algorithm reversed is to invite a mix of donors and potential donors. With a shift in emphasis from immediate fund raising gratification to donor stewardship and friend building, the reception's tone was up-beat and non-adversarial. Board members, staff and long-time contributors were much more at ease, thereby setting a more receptive environment for the cultivation of new friends who over time might become valued donors.

This line of creative thinking is not too dissimilar to my board's contemplations about its relationship with major donors. Trusting donors to respond positively by sending in contributions in weeks following our annual get-together enabled us to rethink what we truly wanted to accomplish with the annual dinner event. As we looked back over attendance and observed a distinct trend of lower attendance over the last three years it became obvious that something must be done or possibly experience eventual extinction. An abrupt shift in our paradigm of thinking was needed. It was simply time to trust our friends.

AHA! CASE INSIGHT

Grizzly bears apparently know about creative thinking, but it is a shame that they haven't done a better job in passing the lessons along. Chris Morgan, a noted conservationist, ecologist and co-director of the Grizzly Bear Outreach Project in Washington State, was filming Alaskan brown bears on the Katmai Peninsula over several weeks. He and his filmmaker, Joe Pontecorvo, continued to cross paths with a sow accompanied by two cubs of the year. Gradually she became comfortable enough with Pontecrovo and Morgan that she would leave the cubs in their vicinity and wander away to forage. Morgan and Pontecrovo took on the role of quasi babysitters. Over the weeks this sow had reversed her algorithm of thinking about the men and in so doing understood that they were good cub-sitters whose presence would automatically fend off large threatening males thereby freeing her to attend to her nutritional needs. She won, her cubs won, and Pontecorvo and Morgan won. Everyone was happy— except the marauding male boars. However, even they won—they simply kept away from the human interlopers.

Four Easy Steps to Achieving Ingenuity

Reversing the algorithm essentially represents a process of unlearning standard thought processes. In many respects it amounts to removing traditional assumptions and constraints that immediately flood our minds when we begin to look at a problem. As simple as it appears on the surface, try following these steps to achieve fresher insights to solutions for that thorny problem you next confront:

1. Concentrate in an extremely focused manner to develop an image of the problem. Decide what the problem is, specifically, that needs to be resolved.
2. Think of the typical way that this problem would be resolved by most people. Even think of very clever ways that people would go about solving the problem.
3. Turn those solutions on their head; flip them 180 degrees; do the opposite; reach an understanding of what the reverse approach would be to the standard solution for any given problem.
4. Look for insightful clues about how the problem can be better solved from these completely reversed ways of thinking about problem solutions.

I wish I could make it more complex than the four steps defined above, but I cannot. The process of following these four steps inevitably provides sparkling ingenious resolutions to the thorniest problems.

When a difficult problem confronts people, their cognitive thought processes tend to direct them to past problems of the same nature. Consequently, as a matter of efficiency, our brains direct us to think about how we previously solved those problems. Unknowingly, we begin to select among suboptimal solutions that offer a good choice; but not the best choice. To achieve successful fund raising we need optimal solutions, not satisfactory ones.

AHA! CASE INSIGHT

Consider the situation I encountered one winter morning when I decided to turn off my sprinkler irrigation system for the season. A valve in the shape of an "X" was spliced into a water line emanating from my house. All I had to do was close that valve and the system was secure for the winter (temperatures were moderate enough to not justify blowing out the irrigation line). Carrying a four-foot long sprinkler handle with an inverted "U" on the end that fit over the "X" pattern of the valve gate, I walked around to the back of the house. A three-inch diameter plastic pipe, three-foot long, provided access to the valve gate.

I reached the plastic pipe; peered down into it and carefully seated the sprinkler tool on the gate. Then I proceeded to shut the valve gate closed. Seconds later after twisting clockwise, the gate closed shut. I extricated the sprinkler tool and peered down into the plastic pipe. Funny…I thought…I think I can see water leaking from the top of the valve gate. I retrieved a flashlight from the house and once again peered down into the plastic pipe. Sure enough…the valve was leaking.

Why does it always take so long to do the simple chores? I knew that the valve would be leaking for months if I didn't do something about it so I resolved right then and there to replace the valve gate. It was too close to the foundation of my house to risk letting water seep there all winter-long. So, I went back to the garage and retrieved a shovel and tarp to lay extricated dirt upon. From there I proceeded to dig a 3'x3'x3' hole to access the pipe and valve gate. Thirty minutes later the valve gate was exposed and the offending trickle of water very apparent as the surrounding soil was already becoming quite saturated.

I did not have the proper tools or parts to replace the valve gate so I opted to throw money at it by calling my plumber, Jerry. He said he could come over the next morning and I spent another 30 minutes making certain all dirt was away from the valve gate and that Jerry could cut through the pipe to make a quick (and low cost) repair.

Twenty-four hours later Jerry pulled up in front of my house. I met him, greeted him jovially and helped lug his tool box to the backyard. I wanted him to fix this in a minimum amount of time since he was working on my dollar. We pulled up to the ginormous pit I had dug. Standing there proudly I mentioned that he should be able to cut the line and insert a new gate pretty easily given the excavation. So...get to it Jerry.

Jerry congratulated me on my artistry with a shovel and then stood there for a few precious minutes looking down on the growing puddle of water that was leaking from the top of the valve gate.

"Looks like it is leaking," he said.

"Duh," I thought to myself. "Get on with it."

More seconds ticked by as Jerry rooted through his tool box.

He stood up with a wrench in his hand.

"Oh boy," I thought. "He is finally going into action."

Next, Jerry turned to me and asked, "Did you tighten the valve gate nut?"

"Valve gate nut? Why of course it has a nut on top," my brain snapped back.

My palms began to sweat.

"Tighten the valve gate nut?" I asked.

"Yes, tighten the valve gate nut," he said as he jumped down into the pit and in one fluid motion secured the wrench on the nut and gave a couple of turns.

"There you go," Jerry said with a smile of satisfaction as he began stepping out of my wondrous pit. "All fixed."

We walked back to his truck and he proceeded to write an invoice for $45. In return I wrote a check and then watched him drive off. Forty-five dollars for about 10 minutes' worth of time was the final verdict.

Now $45 is not significant in the grand scheme of things. But the experience offered a lesson that I would never forget. My algorithm of thinking had cost me plenty. When I saw the leaking valve gate my algorithm of thinking told me to replace the valve since it was defective. I followed that algorithm to its final conclusion. Replace the valve gate by Jerry, my plumber. My thinking followed a logical pattern: valve gate defective; replace offending valve gate.

I never stopped to turn the algorithm around: valve gate leaking; do not replace valve gate. Well how do you stop a leak if you are not replacing the broken valve gate? You repair the valve gate first…and secondly replace it if you cannot fix it. It would have taken only a few seconds to reverse my algorithm and test the efficacy of a more creative (and less expensive) solution.

In the preceding example, the overall cost of following an algorithm was low. But, consider what could have been the outcome if the stakes were a lot higher, such as reaching a hospital's comprehensive fundraising goal.

There is no substitute for ingenious, imaginative thinking.

The Rest of the Story

Given the preceding thoughts about how to inject more innovation and resourcefulness into fundraising it is appropriate to return to the beginning of this chapter. When we left that lucky day where a disconnected coupe of wealth made an unanticipated $2,500 overture, I was in the middle of dialing my colleague. Here is the rest of the story.

My colleague and I had a quick debrief on the lunch. She was pleased that I finally had the opportunity to meet this couple and to get to know them better. But, my colleague was most effusive about our little victory, a gift when one wasn't expected. She began to run down the list of ideas for distributing the gift: 5 allocations worth $500 would touch more clients and have a bigger impact than awarding the entire amount to one person; 2 grants at $1,250 would help identify a couple of worthy candidates and if one did not perform there was always the other to point to; targeting the grants to single mothers because that was a big interest of the female donor; and so the conversation went.

After exhausting her ideas she asked me for my take on the matter. I first congratulated her for doing what no one else had ever done; secure a gift from this family. I also underscored her deft handling of the luncheon. Timing was perfect; the venue conducive to the presentation; and the climate was just perfect; there was no dunning message about how bad off we were due to the economic recession. I also chided her for having butter on her breadsticks. She was a sucker for balls of butter, not that I was in a position to comment given her svelte figure compared to mine.

I hesitated in silence for a couple of seconds and then asked her whether the program supervisor might have any spare change lying around. She did not have an answer but she asked what I had in mind so I went on to explain my conviction that this professional couple was very likely to place great scrutiny over how we expended their initial gift. My colleague concurred. At that point I proposed a plan that immediately would take the relationship to the next level. I explained that if the program supervisor had $5,000 in discretionary funds available, we could go back to the donors and ask them for another $2,500 (for a total of $5,000) to match the funds put forward by the supervisor. The total, $10,000, would qualify for the minimum threshold necessary to establish an endowment for this healthcare foundation.

My colleague understood the charm and insight of this strategy right away. Here was an opportunity to double a totally unexpected gift *and* to establish a new endowment that would prove we were good stewards with the donors' funds. In effect, the gift wouldn't be one-time; it would be in perpetuity. And the endowment could be named thereby recognizing them or a loved one. Plus, further gifting would be that much easier since they could simply give to the endowment to expand its corpus and hence increase allocated earnings that the endowment would kick off every year going forward.

In fact all of the above occurred. The program supervisor did have the funds and he appreciated the long run implications for his program. The donors were overjoyed at the thought of establishing an endowment. We proposed a payout of the $2,500 over a couple of years to minimize sticker shock of a $5,000 gift. Since they had the means, they did not choose a pay-off schedule. The endowment was created and to this day clients are benefitting from the support. The program has a new relationship with two friends that it will continue to build. All of this happened because we took the time to reverse think about how the situation might be better managed to create more value.

Toward Imaginative Better Practices

Following the same old tried and true best practices fundraising strategies and tactics is increasingly difficult given economic constraints and budget reductions. In many cases there is neither staff nor support resources available to get the job done. This does not prevent executives from thinking creatively about achieving those knotty fundraising goals. Ingenuity can flourish. Freed from having to follow traditional models of fundraising, executives can assemble an entirely new model of best practices for the situation or "imaginative better practices" that jibe with the constraints of the situation.

So-called "best practices" can be eschewed for more creative "better practices"; strategies that are often quirky, situation-specific, ingenious and results-oriented rather than guided by common standards in the field. The following ingenious approaches are illustrative of what it means to rethink fundraising.

Short-run Goals have Highest Priority

How often are for-profit corporations criticized for sacrificing long-run goals as short-run profits are maximized? Executive compensation systems typically provide the incentive to maximize short run profits so that executive bonuses are larger. This behavior is generally inimical to long run performance and well-being of an organization. Consider what happens when an organization decides to sacrifice the long-run for the short-run by not hiring an executive director of advancement—a six-figure expense can be averted annually over several years. However, the long-run costs of decreased donations can be alarming because successful fundraising is all about establishing long-run prospect/donor relationships.

Another example of sacrificing long-term aspirations to the benefit of short-run gains is also found in the area of donor stewardship. An organization may make a deliberate decision to *not* invest significantly in the accoutrements typically associated with donor stewardship—glossy reports, fancy events, direct mailings, high-touch outreach—because these resources are better invested in cultivating major prospects. The highest-and-best-use criterion offers a razor-sharp rationale for allocating resources in tight times. This decision to substantially under-fund widespread donor relations may seem heretical, but it is the return from focusing on major gifts that ultimately verifies the value of reversing this algorithm of thinking.

Reversing Best Practices Produces Best Results

The opportunity to completely reverse a perceived best practice, and as a result achieve a better practice, happens more frequently than managers might imagine. This is especially true where a sense of freedom to innovate becomes part-and-parcel of daily operations because top management encourages imaginative thinking.

AHA! CASE INSIGHT

The associate vice president of a large integrated health services venture offering assisted living, in-home care, residential care, retirement housing and senior retirement housing joined her close friend for lunch. The friend was director of a local philanthropic foundation and she invited the associate vice president to submit an application for funding—the foundation had an unexpected $100,000 to allocate and the director's board specified that 10 grants of $10,000 would be made. The associate vice president's friend confided that the foundation was particularly receptive to proposals that might advance nursing care to seniors.

The associate vice president was several weeks out from this foundation's grant deadline and she had to make a decision: would she submit an application for a $10,000 grant; or, would she spend that time cultivating two major gift prospects that were nearing the point of being presented with a proposal to co-fund a $1 million capital renovation project?

The associate vice president thought about the matter and decided to completely forego the $10,000 grant application in order to focus squarely on the top priority. It was a very refreshing moment made all that much more acceptable because her boss, the CEO, had been admonishing the executive team to think out of the box in addressing the overwhelming demands they were confronting given recent staffing reductions.

Four weeks later the nursing director for this integrated care organization learned about this apparent decision to not apply for the $10,000 grant. "How could you not fill out the proposal?" the nursing director asked. "Quite simply," the associate vice president replied. "I just ignored it." The nursing director walked off confident that the associate vice president simply wasn't doing her job. The associate vice president let the matter sit for a few days and then informed the nursing director about enlightened trade-offs. The so-called "best practice" of always following-up with a foundation's invitation to submit a grant application is *normally* a best practice. However, this is one time where the better practice is to focus on the highest and best use of a scarce resource, the associate vice president's time. The associate vice president did inquire about whether the nursing director would like to respond to these grant opportunities in the future, but the nursing director declined because of being too busy.

The associate vice president could sympathize with that response.

Multiple Good Ways to Achieve Excellent Results

A push for best practices tends to generate an obsession with standard formulas for the way things should be done. This logic is very alluring. If the best performers in a field orchestrate their processes and operations in a certain recipe then it would behoove all other contenders to do likewise. Replicate the formula and you should replicate the results. If you do not mimic leaders in the field and your results are substandard, then the burden of proof is on you to demonstrate otherwise.

A formulaic approach to production may be conducive to turning out standardized cookie cutters, cheap motels, identical clone computers and zillions of automobiles, but when it comes to successfully raising friends and funds it is all about the stamp of individuality and tailored relationships. In the end every executive should organize and implement their efforts according to what works best for them, not to how it compares to some prior conception of the one best way to cultivate donors. Autonomy to complete work with your own autograph also carries with it an explicit agreement that the focus is on results.

Aha! Tip: Executives should put their signature on their fundraising strategy because there are multiple good ways to achieve the same end results.

Ideas Du Jour are Seldom Best Practices

Many executives fall into the trap of thinking that any hot idea, one that is gaining significant press, buzz or attention in the media, is an indispensable idea. There is often a blind leap of faith that ideas du jour should immediately be given credibility as best practices. If leading organizations have adopted a practice, then it must pass muster as a best practice. After all, everyone wants to be on the cutting edge of the field. Foresight to quickly embrace innovation certainly must reflect positively on an organization; at least that is the reasoning underlying the fallacy of management fashion trends.

Could there have been any hot topic in fundraising during the past several years that is more engaging than social media? A national presidential campaign was won due to voter fundraising via social media. Various natural disasters in recent times have been at least partially remedied by social media. Several governments have been phased out around the world due to social media. There is no denying that social media offers a very powerful mechanism for galvanizing people in response to significant events.

The report card is much less impressive for social media applications in fundraising. This may result from the lack of urgency attached to messages. It may also be an artifact of donor fatigue to these types of campaigns. Whatever the explanation, adopting a social media initiative does not guarantee successful *short-term* fundraising, at least not at the current state of the art. This good idea may be a very fruitful strategy for the long-run, but evidence from the field of philanthropy suggests that social media has not proven successful in large, episodic capital campaigns.

Standardize Benchmarks

Performance measurement is fundamental to superior execution of strategies and a prerequisite to instilling modifications required for improving attained outcomes. Methodically monitoring performance against a commonly recognized set of benchmarks is a best practice and a management policy that simply makes good sense—except when benchmarks become tyrannical. The highest performing organizations in every field have adopted evidence-based practices and it is an expectation that stakeholders and constituents uphold for organizations or programs that are striving for recognition as one of the best. However, following-the-leader simply to follow-the-leader is never a good idea. Use benchmarks that fit your setting. Adapt them—standardize them—to fit the setting and this will enable your organization to capitalize on the best of benchmarking while also taking into account the uniqueness of your organization's setting.

Lessons to be Learned

In the final analysis, best practices are not a panacea for accomplishing organizational goals. The contextual environment plays an important role in determining what strategies can be implemented and how successful they will ultimately be in terms of outcomes. Thus, a best practice for one setting may be inappropriate for other settings. Although it is easy to jump on the best practices bandwagon, savvy executives and informed board members should be cautious in thinking that best practices are a cure-all for high performance.

Steven Shapiro in his eloquently titled book, *Best Practices are Dumb*, makes a convincing case about foregoing the pursuit of best practices because they tend to overly constrain creativity.[10] He also makes an excellent point about the incommensurability of organizations. Those entities that are well-known for best practices often possess unique assets or enabling factors that are not readily available to other organizations. In essence they have a leg up even before the service or production process begins.

Despite an adverse economic environment, continual innovative thinking about fund raising strategy formulation and imaginative ways to execute strategy are important tools in overcoming what may seem like extraordinary constraints. By continually thinking about ways to cleverly alter strategies and tactics, refinements were instilled that enabled progress toward goal attainment. *Is there really any other better practice than success?* Certainly the best practice is constantly devising ingenious ways to overcome the next obstacle to goal attainment.

It all comes down to this: the philanthropy field needs to push for better practices and at its farthest extension, ultimate innovative practices as far as fundraising is concerned

KEY AHA! POINTS

- Success in fundraising is all about thinking with more imagination.
- A very fruitful way to solve fundraising problems from a more ingenious perspective is to reverse the algorithm of thinking.
- The magical steps in reversing the algorithm include:

  1. Concentrate in an extremely focused manner to develop an image of the problem. Decide what the problem is, specifically, that needs to be resolved.
  2. Think of the typical way that this problem would be resolved by most people.
  3. Turn those solutions on their head; flip them 180 degrees; do the opposite
  4. Look for insightful clues about how the problem can be better solved from these completely reversed ways of thinking about problem solutions.

- In many instances so-called "best practices" can be eschewed for more creative "better practices"; strategies that are often quirky, situation-specific, ingenious and results-oriented rather than guided by common standards in the field.
- Executives should put their signature on their fundraising strategy recognizing that there are multiple good ways to achieve the same end results.
- Remain suspicious about the so-called idea of the day that every organization, every executive, seems

to be adopting. Often these flash-in-the-pan ideas have merit, but not if they are adopted simply because everyone else or every other organization is adopting them.

• The idea of best practices, such as evidence-based decision-making, is a good one, but not if it becomes a formula that hinders more creative problem solving. Adapt benchmarks to fit your organization.

Capturing the Attention of Wealthy People

Ability to capture the attention of wealthy people is perhaps the leading acid test for any executive seeking to raise funds. Normally very rich people have seen it all, heard it all, and been vulnerable to being conned by the very best. Long before we meet them with an innocent intention of sharing news about a noble mission, they have been methodically beaten up by one flimflam artist after another. People with wealth endure these come-ons and eventually they suspect almost every overture as a potential drain on their time and energy. Fundraisers simply want to get into their wallets and bank accounts. Not surprisingly, folks of affluence are not very accessible or attentive. As far as they are concerned, they do not need what we have to sell to them.

Executives may have better success in fundraising if they take the stance that they do not want to sell anyone on anything. This approach is totally different. If an executive has agreed to use valuable time and energy in becoming associated with an organization/entity, then it makes sense that she/he is especially motivated to share her/his organization's mission, purpose, goals, and impact with others. In short, executives want other people to understand why they are ardent champions for their organization.

Internalizing an organization's mission or purpose is palpably essential to successful fund raising. If an executive tries to fake passion for an organization or program; others will notice, especially people of wealth. They can smell a phony from a mile away. And, if that executive tries to sell them something that the executive herself/himself does not believe in affluent people only tend to validate their conclusions about what an executive wants from them.

In sum, a person must have a proper connection to an organization as well as commensurate admiration of its mission in order to be a success in fundraising. If an executive has this base then she/he is in a position to do something about helping an organization, program or entity that is admired. They are particularly positioned to inform people about the good cause for which they have high regard. They are prepared to capture the attention of those with the greatest capacity for helping out—people of wealth.

Once an executive meets the acid test of being prepared (having internalized an organization's mission), capturing the attention of people of wealth hinges on several key actions outlined in Figure 6-1. Not too surprisingly, these actions have significant congruity with fund raising best practices for every prospect or donor. However, there is a very real difference in how carefully these strategies must be implemented and how conscientiously they must be followed when working with people of financial means.

Figure 6-1

Six Keys for Capturing the Attention of Wealthy People

Inform them about a compelling vision or cause.

Validate the vision or mission by using supporting testimonies.

Enlighten them about the results that gifts produce.

Explain how gifts can be leveraged.

Steward their involvement.

Express ongoing appreciation.

Inform Prospects about a Compelling Cause

There are exceptions to every rule, but for the most part wealthy people fundamentally want to invest in very persuasive missions or causes. They do not value a dollar less than other people; in fact, experience suggests that wealthy people actually value a dollar more highly than non-wealthy people. They want to make certain that any dollar they invest is allocated toward a great cause or toward a highly redeeming opportunity. People of means often have worked very hard at earning their wealth or they have exercised substantial effort in retaining their wealth. They are not about to simply give it away.

Wealthy people have the ability to make a huge difference in whether a funding goal is reached, or not. Consequently, it is vital to secure personal introductions that open the way to presentations about your organization's/program's compelling cause. The perceived value to the community or the overall importance of an organization's mission is critical to major donors.

AHA! CASE INSIGHT

For more than a year I had been trying to gain an introduction to a very wealthy gentleman who for the sake of anonymity will be called "Arnold." Lots of people claimed to know Arnold, but they were generally unable to devise a way that we could come together for an introduction. Every time that a friend arranged a luncheon, Arnold was careful to cancel at the last minute feigning a good reason. And truth be told, some of those excuses *were* more than just excuses.

Arnold knew (on a superficial level) who I was and what I represented, but he was not interested enough in my story because, like wealthy people everywhere, he suspected that he knew what I really wanted; to ask him for money. I intensified my efforts in befriending Arnold's friends. If the mountain would not come to me then perhaps someone else would make the mountain move in my direction. And, one year more passed before magic happened.

I received a call from a close friend, himself a person of significant wealth, about rafting a major white water river. This multi-day trip would put us smack dab in the middle of nowhere over four days. I love rafting in gorgeous wilderness areas so this was not a hardship assignment by any means. Best of all, my friend shared the other personalities that would be accompanying us on that trip including a very wealthy couple that I had only begun to know, and Arnold along with his wife. Opportunity was knocking.

We flew into the rugged backcountry in small single-engine planes sharing a perilous encounter with the grim reaper as we landed deep on the banks of a wilderness river. Our launch day was sunny and bright; perfect weather for casually floating this iconic watercourse. With four rafts and one paddle raft the entire party of thirteen people was spread out along the river, occasionally bunching up as we negotiated serious rapids. It was truly a bucolic day. By design I made certain that I did not join Arnold on a raft that first day. I had plenty of time to get to know him better around the campfires and over dinner and breakfast. Patience is a virtue.

The next morning after breakfast we broke camp. Our guides went to their rafts and let the rest of us select which raft they wanted to ride in. As others chose one of the large oar rafts, I went for a small paddle raft. Sitting in the middle with a paddle in hand, I was quite surprised to look up and see Arnold joining us. He took a seat up front and I felt the stars aligning in my favor. The soulful morning that followed was quite tame except for a pestering upstream wind. After lunch a chilly breeze intensified as gusts whipped up small gossamer sheets of spray. Brooding clouds began descending over the white-capped river. When you are in heavily mountainous and canyon country it is difficult to see the general path of a storm or its heft. Not surprisingly, we soon learned that a full-on fall storm was sweeping over our wilderness.

Somehow in the change-out of rafters after lunch I had been pushed up to the front; seated across from me was Arnold. We both took the brunt of small waves slamming over the raft's lip and in effect we served as a sacrificial seawall. Our friends hid behind us whenever things became choppy or wind-whipped. It wasn't long before Arnold was shivering and he casually asked his wife to pass him his fleece shirt. I had already bundled up at lunch so I could only imagine how cold he was.

Arnold's wife inquired about where he put it in the dry sack that our outfitters had passed out to each of us. He looked a bit surprised, and then replied that he thought she had packed his gear. Somehow, someway, Arnold's gear was left at home. Now he was in the middle of a raging wilderness storm with only a paddle. Fortuitously I packed like I always do when expecting extreme conditions. I had packed a fleece shirt as an extra margin of safety, and I had also packed a spare set of paddling gloves. I wish you could have seen Arnold's temperament change once he put that furnace of a shirt on and added my pair of gloves. Both pieces of equipment looked, and were, virtually brand new. That was one satisfied Arnold for the remainder of the day's float.

After reaching camp that night Arnold came over with my fleece shirt and gloves. He wanted to return them. That was silly, of course, because they were spares which I did not need. It did not take much encouragement to convince Arnold that he really needed then more than I and for the remainder of the trip we rarely saw Arnold without that fleece shirt.

Thus, it was not too surprising that at breakfast the next morning as we stood around a flickering campfire, Arnold approached me and struck up a conversation about what my organization was doing these days. The mountain had finally come to me. And, I made the most of it. I only focused on telling the story of a winning program and its distinctive results. I never even remotely talked about funding needs. I simply talked with passion about what we did and what we had achieved.

Two days later as we beached our rafts for the last time and began sorting gear for the return flight home, Arnold moseyed over and tried to return his equipment. I underscored that it was his gear by now and to put them to good use by rafting another river in the future. He thanked me and asked for my business card which I always carry.

Three months later after several meetings, Arnold made a seven figure commitment toward my organization. This was a pretty good return on a $60 investment.

Wealthy people do want to support worthy causes. But, they first have to hear about them. This is a problem when they are inundated with many extended hands all seeking a gift for a noble cause. Consequently, I have learned to keep it short and simple when it comes to communicating the mission/purpose of organizations I represent.

Validating Mission Credibility

While many wealthy donors may see themselves as disaffected onlookers who make decisions based solely on what they themselves think, more often than not they are susceptible to being influenced by what other wealthy people are supporting. Like many things in society, people of means can be influenced by philanthropic fashion trends. They do feel more comfortable making large gifts when they know that other people they admire and/or respect are also making large donations toward a particular cause. This is all part-and-parcel of social status as well as validation that a decision to invest has been scrutinized by others of their means.

A colleague compared this phenomenon to what his community called the "five cigars model." Five families of impressive wealth generally controlled corporate giving in his town. If at least two of the five families supported a cause (through the corporations they controlled), it was reason enough for less influential donors to make a contribution. The *compelling mission* had been validated by at least two of the top five families. They simply feel more comfortable because they believe in each other.

By the same token this propensity for donor congruence can also backfire. If a funding project does not have the right allure, popular sizzle or redeeming attraction, this phenomenon may never materialize, or as one wag said: "Sometimes 'No' happens."

Demonstrable Results from Gifts

All donors want to see results from their investments and the larger the gift, the more that they expect to see a suitable return.[11] It is difficult to discern a tendency among wealthy people to be less rigorous in their expectations for a return from their charitable investing. A dollar means as much, if not more, to people of wealth. This may explain why some donors attain their wealth. They are particularly cautious about giving to causes that do not demonstrate responsible results. In fact, they seem to apply a higher standard of expectations for results. They want to make certain that their gifts achieve the professed outcomes that organizations espouse during the cultivation phase.

Executives must be maniacally attentive to providing donors with hard evidence about the difference that their gifts are making. In one extreme case, I was so driven to demonstrate that things were happening that I returned a gift (albeit within the same calendar year to avoid a messy tax issue).

AHA! CASE INSIGHT

A board of eleven national/international experts had been assembled by my predecessor to guide a new global initiative. Unfortunately, this leader failed to inform board members that they were more than advisory; monetary contributions were also expected as part of their role.

On assuming my new position, I immediately gathered the board together. This required a lot of sophisticated logistics because of travel times involved and I was very conscious about the personal and professional expense these board members were investing. Once that first meeting opened with a delightful buffet breakfast overlooking the immaculate grounds of the meeting center, I began to silently curse my predecessor. These folks believed that they were here to give advice and only give advice. They were counting on me to do the heavy lifting of fundraising for this project. That attitude was a bit unusual because my predecessor had specifically selected each person by virtue of giving capacity and affinity for global issues.

Over the next six months the advisory board continued to hold sway about the direction our global initiative should go. They pontificated freely about the concept and envisioned implementation. It was all quite impressive with crystal clear insights and technically astute strategizing. No matter how I tried to direct the discussion toward financial support, the board was able to evade the matter. Even incorporating the subject in the middle of our meeting agenda did not prevent the chair from bringing new issues to the table that unfortunately resulted in fundraising being tabled. I had done my homework and deliberately worked with the chair to convey the importance of getting the funding issue under discussion. I had primed a couple of other board members about the need for them to speak on behalf of the board rising to the occasion with seed fiscal support. This prior preparation went for naught.

By the end of our third meeting I was about ready to throw in the towel and to disband the board when one member finally spelled it out: "We need to give more than advice here, so I am making a $5,000 contribution to get things rolling." Goodness, you would have thought that he had made a $500,000 gift. Everyone expressed their appreciation and gave him plenty of "atta-boys." But this gesture did not encourage others to step up to the plate. Instead, one member commented: "Well I give through covering my travel expenses to these meetings." This was from a vice president of one of the world's largest consulting firms. A few heads nodded, a few more lame excuses surfaced, and some minutes later we adjourned.

Behind the scenes I continued to personally press the board members for financial support. However, the damage had been done by my successor and the dis-interest of the collective board. They viewed themselves only as an advisor group. Finally, I realized that the opportunity costs of my time demanded that I scuttle the project. I called up the first donor and informed him that because I could not demonstrate proper results with his [meager] gift, I was returning it. That was one of the best $5,000 I have ever spent. It raised my level of self-respect and dignity; ended a non-productive initiative that was headed nowhere despite its meritorious mission; and it served as a lesson about boards that has come back to produce substantive rewards for my organizations and others.

Every time I meet with a major donor and she/he is uncertain about what is happening with their gift, I know that I/we have failed to properly do our job. Often I rationalize to myself that things are in process...and they usually are, but that is precisely the scenario under which an even larger effort should be made to keep donors better informed. How many times during the ugliest jam-packed day are there small intervals of 5-10 minutes before or after a meeting when a short phone call would build a better relationship by sharing information? Even a response that "I'm not certain how the project is progressing but a staff member is looking into it and I will report back to you next week" does a world of good when the alternative is a hollow vacuum.

Leveraging Gifts

Have you ever run across someone who does not like a good deal? Most people seem to relish coming away with a great bargain.[12] From my interactions with wealthy people, I can assure you that they are often ecstatic when they know that their gift is somehow going to be multiplied to make it that much more significant. The only question remains about how that can be accomplished. First the donor must be cultivated to the point of the gift and then imagination must be employed to leverage the gift into something of superior value.

AHA! CASE INSIGHT

Thanks to a Forbes article several years ago on the wealthiest people in the United States, I learned that the 205th richest person in the U.S. was affiliated with our institution. At that time Donald Trump was number 204 in the Forbes ranking. We all know Mr. Trump, but very few people knew number 205. He is that sort of person—self-effacing, brilliant, kind, concerned about helping others, grounded in mounds of common sense, and very frugal. Now all I had to do was meet this person and show him the great work that we had been doing in building a world-class organization.

For more than two years I did nothing but build a relationship. Every couple of months I would fly four hours each way to meet for an hour, share a forty-minute lunch and then turn around and head home. It was an exhausting all day event buoyed by sparkling minutes spent with this phenomenal entrepreneur. Often I would take along colleagues; inevitably they concluded that they inexplicably felt great after listening to this gentleman share insights on the economy and business strategy. He was a wizard at what he did and he had a particular penchant for keeping things at the lowest common denominator. A billion-plus dollar commercial enterprise was managed by a staff of six people.

I did not purposefully approach this cultivation as a two-year endeavor. In fact, I had no preconception of when I would submit a proposal and no pressure to speed things up. We had no special campaign or initiative. These were the best circumstances under which to build a relationship that would last a lifetime. I innocently believed that when the time was ripe, he would rise to the occasion.

Finally after two years I took another trip and things progressed like they always did. We enjoyed each other's company. He brought me up-to-date on his many enterprises. I shared the results of how we had altered our operations due to several suggestions he had made. It was an inspiring visit. Flight connections went smoothly. The next day I was thoroughly exhausted but basking in the glow of interacting with someone of substance who thought BIG in a very practical way.

I drafted a follow-up letter. I thanked him for the time he took to meet with me, the interest he showed in our operations, and his suggestions for improvements that we continued to work on. It was a fairly long letter and by the second page I was finishing up what I had to say when I remembered that a new gifting opportunity had arisen. A foundation decided to match any endowed gift with an equivalent amount. So, I added a very brief three sentences that went something like this:

We haven't discussed any interest you may have in giving [to our organization],but I want to inform you about a new opportunity. A local foundation will match any gift by an equivalent amount. I would be happy to answer any questions you may have in this regard.

That was it. I closed with a cordial note about looking forward to our next visit together.

The following week I received a call from our friend. He walked through the business points I had outlined in my letter, noting a change here or adding a thought there. I was quite happy with the call and prepared to sign off when he paused and said, "And to your last point I am sending you a check for [a large six-figure gift]." Suddenly all of those arduous travel hours were paid off by a huge multiple.

Truth be told, I had never regretted any second of time devoted toward visiting this gentleman. I and my organization had already been amply rewarded.

It was the chance to leverage a large contribution that presented an opportunity that he just could not pass up. He knew eventually he was going to make a large gift. It was a matter of when it would happen. The ability to leverage his gift made all of the difference in the world. Wealthy people resonate with superb bargains. Give them that opportunity to leverage any large gift.

Steward Involvement

Perhaps there is no better way to capture the attention of people of wealth than to integrate them on a continuing basis in the operations of your organization. The key word here is "perhaps." In my experience roughly half of all major donors do not want to be intimately involved in the operations of an organization they are supporting and the other half couldn't be more pleased to have an active role. The only way to discern this is to ask each donor how deeply they would like to be involved (i.e., how much time they would be willing to invest) and to offer a broadly vibrant continuum of exciting options with varying levels of intensity.

> **Aha! Tip:** Donor involvement is good, very good. But it can also be bad, very bad. The best advice is to inform donors about the ranges of involvement and to be crystal clear in learning their intentions before consummating the relationship.

The precise tactics used to include major donors are as variable as the imagination it takes to infuse creativity throughout an organization. Whatever tactics are employed it is essential to avoid any decision-making responsibilities that might jeopardize the tax deductibility of a gift or which would compromise the ability of your organization to make decisions with the degree of arms-length transaction appropriate. The fine-line between control and advice is a difficult one to walk and it is your professional responsibility to inform a donor when that line is crossed.

AHA! CASE INSIGHT

I was cultivating a major six-to-seven-figure gift from a donor that was a paragon of wisdom and generosity. Nonetheless, this donor continued to bargain with very strict expectations regarding several fundamental issues, concerns that should be left to the organization to which the donation was being made. I continued to think of clever ways to meet each issue but in the final analysis one huge constraint remained regarding control.

Regrettably, I finally had to advise the donor that it would be better to set up his own nonprofit organization where he would have a better chance to influence how earnings would be spent on the large endowment he was establishing. I could not in good faith accept his gift because he wanted to attach strings that were not professionally, legally or ethically tolerable. It simply was not worth the aggravation or continuing hovering oversight that the gift would bring along with the potential for a friendship to sour due to his overbearing nature. A compromise could be reached by his establishing a separate nonprofit that would annually allocate earnings to our program. We only had to ensure that funding had a rolling three-year term so that in the event that the external nonprofit backed away, our operations would have time to either raise new revenue or sufficient time to go dark.

Effusive Appreciation and Publicity

Properly saying "thank you" should be a given in this day and age; but it apparently is not. Perhaps this is the result of the laid-back informality accompanying email and social media. That is a good excuse, but it still does not justify assuming that all people accept this informality. They do not; and, age is not the sole predictor of whether they expect courteous, professional behavior.

It might be possible to get away relatively unscathed by failing to express appreciation for small gifts. But, does it make sense to try this approach with a person of wealth who could make the difference in whether your program, campaign or project receives the funding that is necessary to bring it to fruition? However you express appreciation, make certain that first and foremost it fits the donor's predilections. Secondly, do not simply assume away the need to continue with proper etiquette even after the relationship has matured. Let the wealthy donor make the overture or raise the question at a positive moment during an upbeat meeting.

A third issue in properly expressing appreciation pertains to public acknowledgement of gifts. Remember to pre-plan visible naming recognitions, public announcements, celebrations and other events and promotional efforts surrounding such gifts. Continue to circle back to donors for clarification. In the past, several wealthy donors have given gifts and initially indicated to me that they do not want to be recognized. Later when a colleague is publically touted for a gift the prior donor may express disappointment for not receiving equivalent treatment.

Try to control for givers' remorse by persistently, but gently, raising the question until a firm response is received. But, be prepared with a back-up plan for when the donor subsequently expresses disappointment. Normally I hear about such concerns from friends or acquaintances of the donor. I treat these rumors as though the donor has personally expressed them to me. It is seldom ever too late to create a recognition option. And, it is often very easy to bundle several gifts into a very robust recognition thereby giving the donor even more acknowledgment than that received by the peer comparison they have expressed concern about.

KEY AHA! POINTS

- Capturing the attention of people of wealth hinges on several key actions:

    o Inform Prospects about a Compelling Cause
    o Validating Mission Credibility
    o Demonstrable Results from Gifts
    o Leveraging Gifts
    o Steward Involvement
    o Effusive Appreciation and Publicity

- Consistently attend to each of the key actions in working with people of affluence. They are very circumspect about thoroughness and appreciate the effort made to do things in a first-rate manner.

Strategizing for the New Normal

The environment for philanthropy has changed at a draconian level just as it has for all organizations.[13] Many reliable fundraising strategies are being examined for their continued efficacy. What worked for the past eighty years since the last major economic recession is seemingly up for grabs. Amid this environment, donors have become extremely cautious about giving large sums of money because they do not have confidence that their personal wealth is protected for the long run. Nonetheless despite the adverse environment, recent improvement in the economy has encouraged affluent people to be somewhat more optimistic about their giving. It remains to be seen whether non-affluent people will be equally optimistic about their potential giving.

In a nutshell the implications of the often tumultuous economic setting suggest that a host of new, innovative strategies should be considered in going forward. That prospect is more than a little daunting. Few executives have time to conjure up a set of new strategies. Who can afford to tinker with fundraising strategies that may not prove successful over time? Many entities have used up their resilience and now hang on by a thread. The last thing they need is to go experiment with a unique approach to raising funds that may not pan out.

Those who stick their heads in the sand and to blindly continue exactly what they have been doing as far as fundraising is concerned are in for a big surprise. Going forward, executives will be pressed to think entirely out of their conventional paradigm. It appears clear that the old adage, "If you keep doing what you have been doing, you will keep getting what you have been getting," should be replaced with a new line of thinking: "If you keep doing what you have been doing, you will wink out of existence."

The question that every executive wants to know is, "What should I be doing differently in order to position my organization to raise funds in this new normal?" Although no one has a crystal ball to predict a reliable answer to this question, a sensible set of guidelines is not that difficult to construct by using a bit of ingenuity. If ever there was a propitious time for re-thinking what strategies work best in the new normal environment, now is that time. Following are some insights that can be useful in reconfiguring fundraising strategies and tactics given the new environment.

Pockets of Wealth in a New Economy

As the stock market plunged to new lows in 2008-2009 people reacted decisively in their giving. Those who have great wealth stepped back an entire level of magnitude as they saw their assets reduced by a significant multiple.[14] Those who have no wealth and who do not have the ability or inclination to be philanthropic continued as they always have. The large middle and upper-middle classes retrenched on their giving patterns, but their gift amounts often do not classify as "major gifts."

Aha! Tip: Three significant trends emerged in the face of economic recession. First, social media offered a way to raise large sums from $1, $5 and $10 gifts. Second, thousands escaped the recession because they have income from an economic segment that is recession-free. Third many inherited wealth.

The 2008 presidential election demonstrated how brilliantly a social media strategy can work *if* properly orchestrated around a compelling campaign goal.[15] First and foremost, donors were enthusiastically motivated to support a candidate who they believed represented change. President Obama's campaign staff waged an impressive grass-roots effort that galvanized younger voters utilizing technology as means to establish cohesion and to solicit needed funding. One of my staff members explained the charisma factor this way: "The electronic messages I received from the campaign left the impression that as an individual I was critical to the candidate. President-elect Obama's future hung on whether I made a $5 contribution or not. I knew that millions of other people were receiving the same message, but the message left me with a conviction that I could not let him down. Two days later another 'crisis' was shared and the importance of making an immediate contribution of $10 was explained. I gave again, and knew that I would be asked in the very near future to step back up to the plate to give."

Millions of donors came together giving small amounts. The economic recession was in full swing, but these predominantly young donors had little to give. They also had virtually nothing to lose economically. Therefore, a call for a $5 donation was tantamount to asking them to give up a fancy cup of coffee. It wasn't that much of a sacrifice nor did it make an appreciable dent on their standard of living or their long-run wealth prospects. In many respects, they had almost nothing to lose and everything to gain.

Since that historic time, advancement efforts across the nation have been trying to replicate this phenomenal success through social media. We still have a ways to go, and we have confirmed the importance of urgency, of an emergency, as a motivational factor behind giving. Nonetheless, the important point as far as strategies for a new normal is concerned relates to a relatively untapped source of funds. Rather than going to the same major prospects over-and-over again, we should be mindful of raising large sums through electronic grass-roots methods. Social media has a proven history of working under the new normal. You can raise large sums through $1-10 dollar contributions.

A second remarkable change has been in individuals who work in or are owners of businesses that have proven recession-proof. No matter how deep the depression, people still need to eat and to carry out the activities of daily living that imply purchasing often low-end goods and services.[5] The organizations and their owners who produce these goods and services generally have escaped significant adverse impact. A case in point is agriculture. People have to eat. This constant demand has created a more stable foundation for farming and ranching. At the end of the day many of these people benefit financially at a time when comparatively more people are earning less.

A third group of people that have a healthy income despite the recession are those who have inherited wealth. These individuals often do not signal their affluence. In many cases they continue to live a lifestyle that they have known for decades. Their wealth continues to mount, but it is not readily apparent. Although the new rich have capacity, they often do not have a mindset, understanding or motivation to change their giving habits.

Avoid the Fair-weather Friend Syndrome

A friend of mine lives in the southwest and is connected to two major universities within the same state. One she graduated from and the other she was employed at for over thirty years. Clearly her relations with each are richly deep. Nonetheless, she loves one and hates the other. The reason for this difference is not so much what transpired during the years she participated at the universities; it is what has happened since that explains the causal difference between love and hate.

The university from which she graduated constantly treats her as a friend. She receives various newsletters, brochures and letters, uncomplicated and profoundly sincere communications, that tell her about what is happening on that campus. And, each year she receives at least one call from a current student who phones to say hello, to share a bit of news about the college my friend graduated from, and to wish her the best for the season (whichever that may be). Occasionally—not every year— my friend will be contacted, first by a mailed letter and a week later by a phone call. The letter describes a funding need of the college and the phone call follows-up without any pressure ("just calling to see if you received the letter about our initiative in the college and whether you have an interest in it"). A "No I am not interested at this time," is received with as much enthusiasm as if she made a $1,000 contribution. As a result, over the years my friend has given beyond her means and inclination. She is willing to sacrifice to help her alma mater *and her friends*.

In contrast, the university where she worked for all of those 30+ years could only build up enough imagination to annually send a letter asking for more money. During the first year after my friend retired, she responded to that initial inquiry with, for her, a sizeable 3 figure donation. Did she receive a "thank you?" No. There was not so much as a phone call or a letter back in appreciation for the gift. But, there were plenty of annual letters dunning her for another contribution. Today she does not even open a letter from her former employer. In phone conversations she cannot find enough wrong that her former employer is doing; even this institution's most glorious contributions to society are susceptible to her scrutiny and dark criticism.

Two nearly identical organizations should have indelible relations with a long-time friend. One can only mount a "fair-weather" relation. The other understands that meaningful relationships are about more than asking for and receiving money. In the new normal we cannot afford to be sloppy in how relationships are built and maintained. An old maxim holds true: treat others as you would like to be treated.

Target Beneficiaries

Experience shows that organizations routinely forget to focus on those possible prospects below the radar screen that have benefitted most from an organization's presence and contributions. An example can explain this quite handily.

AHA! CASE INSIGHT

The organization I was employed by at the time hired thousands of staff members and delivered services to thousands of clients every day. All day long a portion of those folks walked across the street to have breakfast, lunch and dinner at a local restaurant that was famous for its tasty fare. That restaurant literally made millions off my employer and when it came time to solicit donations, the restaurant's owners were at the top of the list as far as prime suspects because they were an obvious target beneficiary.

It was the Thai restaurant at a difficult-to-reach half-mile away that failed to make it on the major gift prospect list. Any of our staff or clients would have to walk a discouraging half-mile across an enormously busy thoroughfare, and then negotiate a ghetto maze where many shady characters tended to hang out before reaching this backwater storefront. Surrounding buildings reeked of decrepit collapse. If ever there was a façade of a greasy spoon, this restaurant possessed it.

What the Thai restaurant lacked in physical appearance and community elegance, it made up for in scrumptiously wholesome food. People can only eat so many burgers, fries, tacos, pitas, burgers, fries, submarine sandwiches, fries, and burgers before they crave something healthier. And, to top it off, this restaurant offered a killer value—sound portions of delectable entrees (read: less rice and noodles). It was the proverbial best value meal you could get within ten miles of our building. As a result, the cramped dining room was always crowded. I knew many people who delayed their lunch hour to accommodate the hordes trying to gain access for a decent meal.

Over the years I became acquainted with the owner and his wife. They always looked so haggard in stained aprons, hair wildly askew, and dark bags under their eyes. In view of their appearance my heart went out to them. Here were two people struggling to make a go of it in a lousy backwater location floating on a fragile economic sea. I always felt so sorry for them…that is, until one day a few years later when I was shopping at a chic set of stores in a town 60 miles away.

I was bidding my time shopping until my dinner reservation was ready at one of the most trendy fusion restaurants in the region. While looking over some outrageously expensive kitchen gadgets offered by a local cooking purveyor, I glanced out the window. To my surprise, here were the Thai restaurant owners getting out of a 500 series Mercedes. They were very cool in their swanky clothes…I hardly recognized them. It was as though they had visited the best clothiers and hair salons at Hollywood and Vine. When they quickly slipped into the same fusion restaurant I was waiting for, I knew my organization had been had by its own nearsightedness.

Appearances are deceiving. Assume nothing when it comes to who or what benefits from the largess created by your organization's presence and economic outfall. Identify the unlikely targets that every other fundraising entity overlooks. These pockets of prosperity are precisely the advantage that many organizations will need to thrive under the new normal with its legions of growing constraints.

Plow Planned Giving

If ever there was a golden moment to intensify planning giving efforts, it is now. Forces are conspiring to improve the prospects for planned gifts. People who are reluctant to cut away at their current assets may be better predisposed for longer-term giving. A planned gift is psychologically remote. And, in the final analysis you will not be around to spend any wealth that you have left over. Could the economy become much worse than it has been the last four years (forget all about 1929 when you read these words)? So, why not do the charitable thing by committing your children's inheritance to a meritorious cause that you believe in right now? I say this somewhat in jest; but I have run into many donors who for whatever reason feel no obligation to their offspring.

Another trend that argues for planned giving is the inheritance baby boomers have experienced, or will soon experience. Their parents were savers (unlike them) and they stand to acquire significant wealth. This may leave many with a sudden influx of personal wealth that tips the scale toward planned giving. These individuals could resonate with the idea that they can have all of their assets at their disposal now and to pass along a major gift after they have died; assuming that the corpus has not been exhausted taking care of them in their final days. This is a bit like having your cake and eating it too. As a major donor who pledges to leave half of my estate to a noble cause, I can receive the accolades and feel-good aura that goes along with an impressive six-seven figure donation. However, if my estate ends up in five figures that's just the way it went.

Positive Feedback

The new normal—a prolonged time of austerity—arguably may never end. That is what many pundits down at the coffee shop are saying as they stroke their fancy lattes and green teas. Stop any woman or man on the street and ask them how they think the economy will be next year. Chances are that they will issue a pessimistic forecast rather than a positive one. It *has* been depressing since 2008 even with market improvement. What matters most to executives in fulfilling their fundraising role is how they react to their environment.

A large percentage of nonprofit organizations in my community have been all too eager to share their financial plight and doom-and-gloom scenarios for cutting back services as the economic recession deepened. What they did not realize was the average donor was feeling the very same cutbacks...only they did not have anyone to complain to or commiserate with about the depressing state-of-affairs they faced.

Aha! Tip: A message of woe and misery is seldom, if ever, met with a compassionate response by the very same people who are swimming in the identical pond. Why ask someone for a life preserver that they have created and are clinging to if you have not made the effort to fashion your own rescue device?

Stop singing "woe is me" and start sending a constant positive message. There is no need to candy-coat the way things were, but make a concerted effort to share positive news and when pressed about how badly things had gotten, answer truthfully with conviction that you are making the right adjustments. Honesty earns respect from those that were going through the exact same downsizing to meet diminished budgets.

Turn to sharing the good news about innovations and improvements. Recessionary cutbacks provide opportunities to experiment with new strategies that may have been needed for a long time. The tyranny of good times is the tendency to continue doing what you have been doing because you want to continue receiving what you have been receiving. Why fix it if it is not broken?

Positive news about gift impact inevitably underscores the importance of donors making a gift in the first place. Without hesitation you can look donors straight in the eye and verify that without the generous gift they made last year, five years ago, or ten years in the past, you would not be serving as many deserving people. In fact, resources provided by prior gift investments actually go farther toward meeting critical needs. You can honestly proclaim, "thank goodness that you made that gift…it is really paying off in helping others."

In the final analysis, positive news is always better received than negative. Best of all, sharing positive news becomes the precursor of future giving. Positive news is always warmly embraced.

Rethink those Hallowed Assumptions

When strategizing for the new normal, it is essential to consider one of the most common mistakes that organizations—particularly nonprofit organizations—tend to make regarding building a war chest to fund strategic initiatives. Inevitably the prevailing thought among foundations supporting nonprofit entities is to build a huge endowment that covers a steady stream of operating expenses. However, as many entities discovered during 2008-2009, a large endowment can shrink very easily and with it the dependable source of operating funds. Under the new normal it is time to rethink those hallowed assumptions about endowments. Reverse that thinking!

Endowed programs offer an excellent case in point. Many organizations aspire to create endowed funds that cover programmatic expenses. Consider the nonprofit hospital that has two strategic initiatives that it wants an affiliated foundation to create endowments for annual support. For purposes of illustration, assume that the hospital is seeking to attract a first-rate program director for a prenatal and parenting education program and to support technical expenses associated with a new minimally invasive robotic surgery system. The hospital seeks a $1.0 million endowment to cover annual salary supplement and professional expenses associated with the program director, and a $3.0 million endowment to cover the annual technical expenses of the surgery system. The $1.0 million endowment spins off $50,000 in allocable earnings from the foundation and the $3.0 million endowment earns $150,000 in spendable allocation.

Raising $4.0 million is a tall order for many healthcare foundations. In fact, this is an ambitious aspiration that may not be attainable given the recession. How will the hospital solve this dilemma?

A good starting point is to think about what constitutes the opposite of an endowment. What is the algorithm reversed? The answer is: a non-endowment. Thus, the $1.0 million endowment to supplement the program director spins off $50,000 in allocable earnings from the foundation and the $3.0 million endowment to fund technical support for the robotic surgery system earns $150,000 in spendable allocation.

Does the program director really care if the funds are endowed? Not really. She simply wants to receive the annual financial benefit of $50,000. Does the physician heading the robotic surgery initiative care if the funds supporting technical expenses are endowed? Yes, the physician would rather know that the robotic surgery system has permanent financial security, however, sometimes such a benefit cannot be provided. An annual budgetary supplement of $150,000 works whether it is from an endowed or non-endowed source.

By rethinking hallowed assumptions, the hospital can make substantial progress toward supporting the prenatal and parenting education program and the robotic surgery system at a time when funding prospects might otherwise appear to be rather dismal. Consider the difference in these two approaches—endowed versus non-endowed funding over a three-year period:

Non-Endowed Positions

Prenatal & Parenting Program Annual Costs = $50,000
Robotic Surgery System Annual Costs   = $150,000
Total per year   = $200,000

Endowed Positions

Prenatal & Parenting Program
   Endowment Costs   = **$1 million**
Robotic Surgery System Endowment
   Costs   = **$3 million**
Total corpus to be raised   = **$4 million**

If you were responsible for raising funds for this hospital during a tough economic recession would you rather be responsible for raising $200,000 per year or for raising $4,000,000? The answer is self-evident especially considering that as far as the staff members are concerned; they simply want the annual funding to run their programs.

Consider the matter from the perspective of donors. Are donors more able and willing to make an annual gift totaling to $200,000 to cover program costs or are they more receptive to a request for $4 million to establish the endowments? Again, the answer is self-evident. And, I would submit that ultimately the non-endowed short-run strategy during a time of recession is healthy for donor relations. It allows donors to make bite-size commitments (Yes; I am willing and able to donate $200,000 each year for a period of time) when they are especially pressed financially (No; I cannot donate $1 million or $3 million at this time). It predisposes them to continuing communications about a financial commitment.

After the donors agree to an annual (non-endowed) commitment, they can be approached each year to ascertain whether they are now fiscally flush. If they are in a better financial position, then it is time to have that discussion about creating an endowment. If they are not flush, the probabilities are extremely good that *at a minimum* they will re-commit to another term gift. Once again the stage is set for a discussion some years later about establishing an endowment. Consequently, this reverse algorithm strategy is excellent for both hospital and donor alike. It may not build endowments at a time of extreme economic constraints, but it may build stronger long-run relations by helping donors at a difficult time for them and their pocketbooks.

The Alarm Clock is Ringing

In case you missed it, the alarm clock is ringing. It is time to wake up; to start thinking differently when it comes to the new normal. Perhaps it is easier to look at things this way: the terrorist attacks in New York City and Washington, D.C. on September 11, 2001 are more than a decade in the past. In the intervening years, travelers worldwide have been inconvenienced by new security regulations. Those regulations are not going away and the carefree days of lax security are history. By the same token, the economic heyday leading up to 2007 appears to be a thing of the past. Every day since the global recession gained steam is yet another day with confusion about which way the economy is headed.

It is time to stop our wishful thinking and patient watching for the reappearance of the way things were several years ago. Perhaps those halcyon days will return. More than likely it will be a long time before they surface again…if ever. The implications for fund raising by nonprofit organizations are very vigorous. The time has come to think differently about fund raising and to lead the way with imagination for fund raising in a new global context.

KEY AHA! POINTS

- The implications of an often tumultuous economic setting suggest that a host of new, innovative fundraising strategies should be considered in going forward.

- There are new pockets of wealth that healthcare executives can target: social media offers a way to raise large sums from $1, $5 and $10 gifts; thousands escaped the recession because they have income from an economic segment that is recession-free; and, many inherited wealth.

- In the new normal executives cannot afford to be sloppy in how donor relationships are built and maintained. Treat others as you would like to be treated.

- Organizations routinely forget to focus on those possible prospects below the radar screen that have benefitted most from the munificence surrounding service delivery.

- Planned giving may have reached a golden moment. People who are reluctant to cut away at their current assets may be better predisposed for longer-term giving.

- A large percentage of nonprofit organizations are too eager to share their financial plight and doom-and-gloom scenarios for cutting back services. Start emphasizing positive messages.

- Under the new normal it is time to rethink those hallowed assumptions about endowments. Reverse that thinking and focus on current—as opposed to endowed—funding.

References

Chapter 1

[1]Jeff Zeleny & Megan Thee-Brenan. *The New York Times*. New poll finds a deep distrust of government. October 25, 2011. http://www.nytimes.com/2011/10/26/us/politics/poll-finds-anxiety-on-the-economy-fuels-volatility-in-the-2012-race.html?_r=1&ref=newyorktimespollwatch&pagewanted=print.

[2]Queenie Wong. *The Seattle Times*. State budget cuts put extra burden on nonprofits. April 20, 2011. http://seattletimes.nwsource.com/html/localnews/2014817764_charities20m.html.

Chapter 2

[3]*Guidestar*. Charity fundraising results see no change in first half of 2011: Nonprofits continue to face difficult post-recession environment. September 29, 2011. http://www2.guidestar.org/rxa/news/news-releases/2011/charity-fundraising-results-first-half-2011.aspx.

[4]Lawrence Henze. Raising money during challenging times. *Blackbaud*. April 2011: 1-8. https://www.blackbaud.com/files/resources/downloads/WhitePaper_RaisingMoneyDifficultTimes.pdf.

[5]Chuck Bartlebaugh. Center for Wildlife Information. Be bear aware. Site accessed December 6, 2011. http://www.centerforwildlifeinformation.org/BeBearAware/BearEncounters/bearencounters.html.

Chapter 3
[6]R.L. Osborne & S.S. Cowen. High-performance companies: the distinguishing profile. *Management Decision.* Vol. 40, no. 3, 2002:227-231

Chapter 4
[7]The Corporate Executive Board Company. The new high performer. *Sales, Marketing and Communication Practice.* 2009. https://sec.executiveboard.com/Public/Files/SEC_New_High_Performer.pdf.

[8]R.J. House. A path goal theory of leader effectiveness. Administrative Science Quarterly, Vol. 16, no. 3, September, 1971.

[9]C.E. Bogan & M.J. English *Benchmarking for best practices: winning through innovative adaptation.* McGraw-Hill, New York, 1994.

Chapter 5
[10]S.M. Shapiro. *Best Practices are Stupid.* Portfolio/Penguin: New York. 2011.

Chapter 6
[11]R. M. Schindler, The excitement of getting a bargain: Some hypotheses concerning the origins and effects of smart-shopper feelings. *Advances in Consumer Research* Vol 16, eds.

[12]Thomas K. Srull, Provo, UT : Association for Consumer Research, Pages: 447-453.

Chapter 7

[13]J.W. Mayo & C.H. Tinsley. Warm glow and charitable giving: Why the wealthy do not give more to charity. *Journal of Economic Psychology*. Vol. 30, No. 3. June 2009, Pages 490-499.

[14]W.G. Mangold & D.J. Faulds. Social media: The new hybrid element of the promotion mix. *Business Horizons*, Vol. 52, No. 4, July-August 2009, Pages 357-365.

[15]C. Zook & D. Rigby. How to think strategically in a recession. *Harvard Management Update*, Vol. 6, No. 11, November 2001.

About the Author

Howard L. Smith
is Dean of the College of Business at Pacific University in Forest Grove, Oregon. Prior to this position he served as Vice President for University Advancement at Boise State University and he is the former Dean of the College of Business and Economics. From 1994 to 2004 he was Dean of the Anderson Schools of Management and School of Public Administration at the University of New Mexico. He was also Director of the Program for Creative Enterprise and held the Creative Enterprise Endowed Chair. The author of 11 prior books, Smith has published over 240 articles on topics in health services, organization theory/behavior and strategic management in journals such as *Academy of Management Journal, Health Services Research, Health Care Management Review and the New England Journal of Medicine.*

www.ingramcontent.com/pod-product-compliance
Lightning Source LLC
Chambersburg PA
CBHW071914200326
41519CB00016B/4617